Sandra Holt is a former c〈...〉
living in rural Aberdeenshire 〈...〉
Church of Scotland congr〈...〉
director, she divides her tin〈...〉
the Spiritual Exercises of Ignatius or Loyola, working
Church of Scotland's Board of Ministry in the selection of candidates for ministry, and writing. Sandra is a columnist for the *Sunday Herald* magazine and for *Woman Alive* and is a contributor to *Inspiring Women Every Day*. She is the author of *Intimacy Human and Divine* and *Listening to the Soul*, both published by SPCK.

# Make Decisions that Matter

## Discerning God's Hope for Us

Sandra Holt

First published in Great Britain in 2004 by
Society for Promoting Christian Knowledge
Holy Trinity Church
Marylebone Road
London NW1 4DU

British Library Cataloguing-in-Publication Data

A catalogue record for this book is available from the
British Library

ISBN 0-281-05587-4

1 3 5 7 9 10 8 6 4 2

Typeset by Avocet Typeset, Chilton, Aylesbury, Bucks
Printed in Great Britain by Bookmarque Ltd, Croydon, Surrey

# Contents

———◦◦◦———

# Introduction

What are the decisions that matter in life? Most of us would agree that those concerning home, family and work are the most important decisions made by the majority of people. Where to live, how to make a living, who to make a home with and whether or not to have children matter because we, and the people who matter most to us, have to live with these decisions, or with their consequences, for a long time. But life weaves an infinity of options into our story, giving us many thousands of opportunities to work and play with our innate ability to choose. These are as varied as which wallpaper to decorate with, which school to send our children to, and how to respond to a crisis when it threatens health, relationships or employment.

Making decisions is part of every dimension of life. But if we have never thought about the process we use, we may have overlooked some prerequisites and neglected to develop some simple skills that will help us to decide well. Choosing is a process that varies from person to person depending on how we think about ourselves, how we see life, and where God fits into our philosophy.

Perhaps we listen to our conscience. It carries strong messages about right and wrong and about ourselves as good or bad people. Strong guidelines may be clear, but are not always helpful. Our conscience often gives the same kind of advice to us as our mother or father might, or some other influential adult who was around during our early development. We may find ourselves strongly inclined to take this advice or equally inclined to ignore it – depending on the relationship we enjoyed with our parents. For many, God is the influential parent, but conscience is not always or exclusively the 'voice' of the heavenly Father either.

We may intuitively apply our personal one-line philosophy of life to the decision. Some Christians wear T-shirts and jewellery displaying the letters 'WWJD' to remind them and encourage the rest of us to consider 'What would Jesus do?' in a particular situation. Few would claim to be perfectly in tune with the mind of Christ but I wonder how many of us detect the presence of other philosophies mixed in with and influencing our Christian response. Hedonists believe that life is for enjoying. The Buddha suggested a philosophical acceptance that life is difficult. Lifestyle gurus would have us believe that life rewards the bold; if a door opens to us and if we are in any way attracted to what the opportunity offers, we should go through it, trusting that however things work out will be for the best, or that one door will lead to another.

A more methodical and cognitive approach begins by applying our intelligence to the facts. We find out as much information as we can about the alternatives and weigh the pros and cons of each to see which decision is most reasonable in the light of these. Perhaps we will consult our friends or colleagues and also our own feelings. We then decide and, if there is time, we sleep on that decision to see how it affects us.

Elements of all these approaches are brought together effectively in the guidelines for Christian discernment offered to the Church over 500 years ago by St Ignatius of Loyola. The very practical approach to prayer and decision-making that Ignatius developed is the inspiration for this book. I resist the temptation to quote from Ignatius' work more than once or twice. Partly this is because lots of other books give a rule-by-rule analysis of his Spiritual Exercises and anyone interested in Ignatian spirituality will want to read some of these. I am more concerned to encourage you to do what he did. Ignatius developed his guidelines and exercises from personal experience of praying with passages of Scripture, especially the Gospels. Christian discernment is of use to those who believe that in each situation of choice between good things God invites us to discover and choose that which is most helpful to the kingdom. But note that God does not compel us to choose this. The will of God in any situation is a non-necessitating preference which can be discovered by contemplating God in action, incarnate in the life, death and resurrection of Jesus and present in our own experience through the Holy Spirit. It can seem a bit of a paradox that God gives us free will in order to let us discover the divine will and choose it if we want to. One of the things I hope to do in this book is make some sense of this mystery.

Discernment turns out to be both an art and a science. When we discern we use method to sift through our feelings so that we can discover the feeling that we have for God. We apply the standards of the gospel to help us uncover our pre-conditioning and prejudices. We examine our motives in the light of Christ's revelation and the truth that will set us free from our fears. Christian discernment is done not by applying a philosophy, or trusting our conscience, or finding out the facts and thinking deeply about them, but by bringing our whole selves to the task in a prayer for self-knowledge and a deep awareness of the creative God who is present in every decision.

God is keen to have us exercise our free will extensively because it is through the creative decisions we make that we become our true selves – perfectly human and equal partners with our creator God. In each decision there are two free wills at work in a partnership of equals: mine and God's. Why, then, do life choices feel more like fiendishly devised tests than occasions for joyfully and confidently expressing our freedom and responsibility as people made in God's image to enjoy life?

For a lot of Christians the problems begin with their image of God and self. We are told to find God's will in a situation, but it is difficult to glimpse God's will for your life if you are under the impression that you are a miserable sinner and God is like a jaded schoolteacher testing your abilities and waiting for you to disappoint. Which is why in this book I am concerned to present both God and man in a different light from the one in which you are perhaps accustomed to making decisions.

When I speak of God's will for you I really mean God's hope

for you. God wills only good for you, but sometimes we think that God is deliberately making life as difficult as it can be. When we try to discern God's will for us we come to the task gloomily, assuming that God will ask us to do the very thing we least want to do. When we think about God in new ways, we discover that God is full of hope for us – and that this is not wishful thinking, but joyful confidence in the whole enterprise of creation.

Our image of God and our fear of 'God's will' may not be all that undermines our ability to make good decisions. It is almost certainly true that our innate skill has been weakened in an age when force-ful marketing encourages us to choose without reference to anything other than our immediate personal desires. We choose because we are told by those selling us the idea that choice is the right of every consumer, but do we choose freely and responsibly?

With all of these difficulties it will not be surprising if we have made some decisions we regret; and painful experiences may have taught us to distrust ourselves so that we avoid making deci-sions whenever possible.

This book offers practical help by engaging you, through examples and exercises, in a personal excavation of the things you believe about the purpose of life in general and your life in particular. It will help you design your own set of tools for discernment and invite you to apply them in issues affecting the global community, personal relationships and the discovery of your unique identity – the person who God is lovingly creating with every decision you make together.

In it I am going to be doing a lot of writing about God, so let me address a frustration I have with the English language. A missionary friend tells me that in Thai there is a pronoun for divinity. In English we have pronouns for male, female or object. I think an opportunity was missed here at the Millennium; we could have created a pronoun for God. Since we didn't take advantage of this opportunity, I will use he/she as often as seems appropriate without being too clumsy. I hope this is a decision that meets with your approval; but, if not, at least you will under-stand why I made it.

# 1

# *God Makes a Decision*

*The glory of God is man fully alive; moreover man's life is the vision of God.*

(St Irenaeus)

My friend Alan is great company and nothing delights me more than to catch up with all his news. Usually this is over a meal in a restaurant – which is fun, except that Alan has enormous difficulty choosing from any menu presented to him. He takes a long time to study each offering and an even longer time to focus on just one. Then he will talk of other things until the waitress approaches, who has taken the abandonment of the menu as a sign that our table is at last ready to order. Suddenly my friend clutches the menu again, his face showing the full agony of his dilemma as he returns to the task. The waitress waits, pen poised over notebook. Finally, with a sigh and sometimes even a mop of his brow if the menu has been particularly impressive, my friend plumps for his choice and with palpable relief relinquishes the menu. I sigh too, for we have only chosen the entrée to our meal and my friend still has not settled on whether or not to have soup – and, if so, which one. The main course is a decision beyond that.

Alan's dilemma is simply stated. To choose one dish will deny him all the other equally inviting alternatives. Any choice will be good, of course, for we are sitting in a fine restaurant, but all of them – while impossible to conceive of digesting or paying for – might be better.

For Alan, and any like him, it will come as some relief to know that though life itself can seem like an à la carte menu, in reality there is only one decision that *really* matters and it is not ours to make. Plenty of decisions *are* ours and we make them every day. What we eat for breakfast, what we wear, how we travel to work, what we do when we arrive there: are all decisions we make daily and unhesitatingly. We have made these same decisions many times and probably varied little in our choice of food, clothes, transport and tasks. This is partly because our choice in each category is limited by previous decisions as well as circumstances. What to eat for breakfast is limited by the earlier decision of what to buy in the supermarket. What we do at work is proscribed by our job description and remit. How we travel to work may depend on the options our earlier choice of home and workplace have provided, or on circumstances like health. Perhaps we can walk, cycle, hop on a bus or take a train. Perhaps the only option available is the car.

Though most of us have no difficulty in making many thousands of decisions of this sort, we take more time over those whose effect lasts longer and extends further than our choice of breakfast cereal does. The decision to change job, home or partner feels more significant than what colour of shirt to wear today. There seems to be more at stake. That's not to say that those little oft repeated decisions have no impact: not eating a good breakfast can make me grumpy and less efficient by mid-morning just when I need all my energy and tact to deal with a client who may also have skipped breakfast. A lifetime of the more sugary cereals, as part of a generally unbalanced diet, will result in health problems affecting not only my own life, but the lives of those around me and, through the demands I make on the health service, the larger community. Nevertheless, we do not lose much sleep over these daily issues as we may do when faced with more material choices.

In one sense every decision we make matters to some extent and a lot of our decisions matter more than we realize at the time we make them. So what is that one decision that really matters?

'In the beginning God created the heavens and the earth' (Genesis 1.1).

Creation is the one decision that really matters because right now, as you read these words, it absorbs God totally. Perhaps you are used to thinking of it as a decision done and dusted in the distant past, but now remote to the aspirations and practicalities of your life. Think again. The decision to create is ongoing, up close and personal to us. God's decision is a story still being written and we are the characters whose own choices carry the plot forward to its completion.

We play our part by making decisions that matter. For a decision to matter it must matter to God. It must be material to the only concern God has, to the one decision God has made. Think of some decisions you have made in the past week. Those that matter will have three characteristics in common. A decision that matters is one that is put into action. If I decide to give up smoking, but never get around to actually doing this, my decision does not matter. A decision that matters is one that makes a creative contribution, not just to my present life but to the lives of everyone it touches directly or indirectly now and in the future. This is difficult to assess since none of us can see into the future. However, we can learn to discern when a decision that promises some good in the short term is likely to disappoint over the long term. Eating a second helping of dessert may give me a lot of pleasure for ten minutes, but the inches added to my waistline and the cholesterol added to my arteries do not come as a surprise. A decision is like a stone thrown into a pool whose ripples extend for ever. That is why the third characteristic of a decision that matters is so important: a decision that matters is a spiritual decision – that is, one prompted by the Holy Spirit who moves over the Earth to complete God's creation. How many decisions have you made in this past week that you can say with some confidence matter to God? How many were what I will call neutral decisions – ones that do no harm but don't add anything to creation? And how many won't matter because though they detracted from God's creation, their influence will prove immaterial in the long term?

## PAUSE AND REFLECT

Think of one decision you made in the past that you are still glad you made. Perhaps it was a change of career or the choice of a partner, or just the decision to take driving lessons. Try to recall as much as you can of the circumstances surrounding the decision. Perhaps you were not sure if it was the right decision at the time; confirmation is often a long time coming, and can seem a nebulous reassurance even then. Remember how you implemented it. Notice the people and situations affected by your decision both directly and indirectly over the years. What is it about this decision that stands the test of time? One decision leads on to another of course, but whatever came after, whether joy or sorrow, my guess is that you know as you look back that your choice is part of who you are now. It is integral to your life and part of the journey you are taking through it.

Not every decision we make is like that, and time and again we make decisions we live to regret. I have made too many to count. Recall a decision that makes you sigh as you remember it. It seemed a good idea at the time, so try to work out what has changed your mind. How did the circumstances surrounding the choice differ from those in effect when you made that other, still peaceful, choice? Often it is not identifying the right course of action that causes us difficulty, but choosing to put it into action. How true was that for you in this situation?

To help us make the kind of decisions that matter in life we need to understand something of God's motivation for creation. God's decision to create mattered because it was prompted by God's own Spirit; it was put into action and it remains creatively relevant for every person and for all eternity.

God created out of choice, not necessity. Some 5,000 million or so years before men were inspired to write the book of Genesis, God was all there was; infinite and eternal. But God was not all there could be. God's decision to create was a decision to share eternity, and this meant squeezing up to make room. This will make a great deal of sense to women who also make room for creation during nine months of pregnancy. Organs are nudged from their natural position and squeezed into a smaller space so that life can grow in the womb. The 'womb' God provided was filled with what we call primordial matter; divine and fecund. From it, gradually developed the cells necessary for creation. These were independent of God while remaining flesh of her flesh because God moved over, but like any mother did not move away.

Imagine yourself entering a packed railway carriage as you travel to work. There are no seats to be found so you stand for some miles until one person beckons and moves over, squeezing into a tight corner, to let you sit down. Imagine your relief and gratitude. Such small acts of kindness from a fellow traveller can have a considerable impact on the rest of our day. They remind us of our own worth. They fill us with hope and energy. They can even make us determined to be generous to others with our time, talents and money. All this can transpire from one simple act of kindness. How might God's decision to move over and make room for you affect the way that you feel about yourself and the choices you make?

God moved over and gave room. It is the only decision that really matters – an act of infinite generosity and compassion motivated by love. Turn the phrase over in your mind as you might turn a smooth pebble in your hand. Get a real feel for the idea. Notice what surprises you, what is attractive or disturbing. Now since God was all there was before creation, who was the subject of God's love?

Christianity teaches that the initiative to create was taken by the one and only living God, and paradoxically that it was a community decision. The belief in God as Trinity, 'three persons in one substance', is a difficult concept for most of us to get our one head around. I like to imagine three folk talking animatedly together in an exuberant Jacuzzi. A more traditional and helpful water analogy is the picture of a mountain spring of crystal water bouncing downhill. There are three distinct elements to notice: the spring, the water, and the flow of that water. Wherever the water flows it brings life to the land and the spring is the source of that life, the water is its substance, and the flow is its energy. In a similar way, Father, Son and Holy Spirit are distinctly three while at the same time being inseparably one.

For nothing comes between these three. There are no power games here; nothing to have but one another, and no threat of loss or separation. The God who moved over to make room knows in his/her own being what it is to be at ease, to have a sense of belonging, to be fully known and understood. So much so that though there are three there is only one: one perfect desire, one expressed will, one unifying energy.

While water is a useful analogy to help us imagine the Trinity we need a more effective model to help us relate to our tri-une God. J. R. R. Tolkien wrote his story of a dark lord's powerful ring and the fellowship who challenged might with mercy, from a deep Christian faith. He agreed with Irenaeus who, in the second century, wrote that God created humanity incomplete but with the potential for perfection. This potential could be realized through a process of moral and spiritual growth. Tolkien also understood life as a quest in which we are perfected through our choices, both those that we make in good times and those that test our character and faith. Through Peter Jackson's films Tolkien's trilogy is now being discovered by millions of film-goers. Whether or not they share Tolkien's faith they have been given, in the story of this fellowship, a very accessible idea of what God is like.

Tolkien did not approve of allegory, believing that it robs the reader of the freedom to encounter their own truth in a story, so let's not look for direct correlation between *The Lord of the Rings* and the story of God's creation and redemption of the world. We can simply allow the characters of Gandalf, Aragorn and Sam Gangee, who support the ring-bearer throughout his quest, to surprise us with new and helpful ways of relating to that other trinity: Father, Son and Holy Spirit.

Gandalf is infinitely wise and amazingly powerful, confounding all with his magic. When a choice of route has to be made, the whole company quite naturally looks to him to make the difficult decision. Gandalf, however, moves over from his position of authority, telling them that it is for the ring-bearer to decide.

Aragorn, heir of kings, makes his first appearance in the tale as a mysterious ranger whose presence disturbs ordinary Shire folk. A man acquainted with sorrows, living on the fringes of society, he humbly looks for friendship, and offers to Frodo his sword and unswerving loyalty for the trial ahead.

Sam Gangee is a hobbit as uncomplicated as they come. His devotion to Frodo takes him to the very crack of Doom and on the way his gentle constancy gathers strength; his will hardens until nothing will separate him from his friend – not the trials of the journey, nor the apparent hopelessness of the grim struggle ahead.

What a formidable trinity these three characters make! In fact, the Trinity of divine persons is at least as impressive and each one is intimately concerned about us. Paul is quite sure that 'neither death, nor life, nor angels, nor principalities, nor things present, nor things to come, nor powers, nor height, nor depth, nor anything else in all creation, will be able to separate us from the love of God in Christ Jesus our Lord' (Romans 8.38–9). This love surrounds us on our journey through life, but perhaps we have not noticed the trust, loyalty and encouragement offered to us at every step and every moment of decision.

## PAUSE AND REFLECT

Each time you spend time in prayer, begin by reminding yourself of this loving fellowship who, even as you turned your thoughts to prayer and your steps to a quiet place, moved over to make room for you within their circle of care.

Take some time to recall the story of your faith, perhaps writing down the bones of it. Remember the people who are, or have been, fellow travellers. The Church is a fellowship of companions who are on a quest together. It is a band of men and women, boys and girls, all of them as different from one another as elves are from dwarfs. Each one is a 'ring-bearer' and each one a companion. The Church is (or could be!) a place where people make room for one another, encourage each other, journey with one another. Is that your experience?

Identify, if you can, the people you have met who have been, for you, a bit like Gandalf, Aragorn or Sam Gangee. Notice the decisions you have made which, whether or not they turned out well, played an important part in your trial and quest. Look for chapters in your story where you encountered (and were perhaps surprised by) God's roominess.

God the Father, Son and Spirit neither dictate your every move nor hover in the background of your life, biting nails in case you take the wrong turning. The God who meets you in your own story is engaged with you, trusts you, and accompanies you with unswerving loyalty, encouraging you when weary and giving you the will to go on making creative choices even at those times of greatest difficulty.

The essence of this one God is love that is relational. John Macquarrie gives us a new way of expressing the little we can grasp about this relational love when he speaks about God as Being. Since Being is simply letting-be, Macquarrie suggests that the essence of God is to let-be. God is love in relation; Being that moves over and lets-be. If it were not so, we could know nothing about God for we *are* those beings that God moves over to make room for.

## PAUSE AND REFLECT

Remember a relationship once enjoyed by you but now broken. What did you share with this other person? Perhaps some of the following: a house, children, aspirations, a business, a recreational pursuit, a faith or a set of values. What did each of you decline to share with the other? The point is not to judge either yourself or the other person, but simply to notice where these boundaries took shape. What did you let be and what could you not let be? I do not share my husband's enthusiasm for amateur dramatics. I do, however, attend the productions he is in and love to see his enjoyment of being on the stage. I let him be all of himself, which includes being a bit of a ham.

It was this letting-be that prompted God to move over and make room for creation. There was no biological clock insisting on the birth of heaven and Earth before it was too late. No instinct for the perpetuation of the divine being motivated the creative act. The Father, Son and Spirit were not looking for more company or a bigger choir to sing their praises. God did not lack anything or have any need or appetite for more. God is love and therefore understood that love kept safely within an exclusive relationship is not perfect for long. Love that is restricted to a few cannot be infinite. Love contained must alter and eventually diminish. Limited love is less than wholly generous, less than sacrificially creative; it is vulnerable and eventually fearful. Love that does not ceaselessly let-be is not God, just as a river that does not flow is not a river.

Love like this does not end with creation. God who is unity envisions an even greater unity and risks all to let *it* be. This unity is the commonwealth of free responsible beings that the New Testament calls the kingdom of God. It's the only thing on God's mind. The one concern that God wishes to share with us and the one true measure of every decision we make.

A proper understanding of this is the key to Christian discernment. God's vision of the kingdom of God, a commonwealth of love, is God's passion and our quest. The love we experience in our families and among our friends and express in our music, art and science confirms this. The Jewish scholar Abraham Joshua Heschel writes:

> The vision of the unbroken ray above the water, the craving for unity and coherence, is the predominant feature of a mature mind. All science, all philosophy, all art are a search after it. But unity is a task, not a condition. The world lies in strife, in discord, in divergence. Unity is beyond, not within reality. We all crave it. We are all animated by a passionate will to endure; and to endure means to be *one*. (Heschel, 1951)

When I am in love I want the whole world to be in love. I wish everyone could feel as happy and fulfilled as I do, as full of expectation and hope for the future. Or when I am passionate about truth and justice I will dare much, endure much to spread my passion, and ignite others with it until the world is transformed. We feel this way because love is not only outgoing and inclusive, but it weaves a work of unity in and between our lives. It is the ultimate freedom to go beyond the boundaries of self and unite with others.

But most of us are not that free. Not many of us change the world with our love, though love is the only power that will do the job and is in infinite supply. God moves over to make room, but instead of stretching into the roominess we remain cautious and exclusive in our own decisions. Partly this is because we think that freedom is the right to make decisions for ourselves. We seek to increase this freedom by adding to the number of decisions in life that we can make. But quantity does not guarantee quality, and often expanding our own freedom means restricting the freedom of other people. This is not the freedom God has in mind. It is not what God is creating. Real freedom is communion with God. It is being part of the unity enjoyed by the Trinity and extended to us.

One of the stumbling blocks to the freedom that transforms is religion. Many of us worship a very different God to the Trinity of loving roominess presented here. We imagine creation not as a compassionate conception, but a royal decree: 'Let there be light' (Genesis 1.3). It sounds imperious because it is, conveying sovereignty and power. Once this imperious figure appears on stage, however, many find it difficult to get him back off again. He struts through history, pointing out our failings and disobedience, and forcing us to hide from him as Adam and Eve famously did after pilfering fruit in the Garden of Eden. It seems we believe that Adam's decision to eat the apple was more momentous than God's decision to create both Adam and the apple in the first place! We have learned that his power is absolute and his word is law. He decides right from wrong, good from evil, sacred from profane. He expects his helpless, hapless children to be seen (doing God's will) and not heard (to question it). Indulgent towards us – at least when we are obedient – he shuns us when we rebel, alternatively threatening and coaxing us back on to the straight and narrow path of divine favour. He loves us we are sure, but he loves his honour more. What in human affairs matters to this demanding patriarch? It is difficult for his children to know for sure because the messages from him are mixed. And have you noticed 'he' is male?

We might as well face it: these mixed messages appear in Scripture or have been developed from Scripture. Perhaps the most difficult and the most damaging to the psyche is the incredible notion that God selects some of us for salvation before we are born and consigns others to destruction. This doctrine (predestination) was developed from a hypothetical question Paul raises in his letter to the Church at Rome:

What if God, desiring to show his wrath and to make known his power, has endured with much patience the vessels of wrath made for destruction, in order to make known the riches of his glory for the vessels of mercy, which he has prepared before-

11

hand for glory, even us whom he has called, not from the Jews only but also from the Gentiles? (Romans 9.22–4)

## PAUSE AND REFLECT

Do you believe in this arbitrary God without even knowing why? Is the God you worship like the fellowship that surrounds Frodo and helps him to free Middle Earth? Or is he a bit like Sauron, whose flaming eye seeks out in order to destroy any will opposed to his own? Are you trying to make decisions that matter to this tyrant? Check it out by noticing how this passage from Jeremiah, used by Paul in the same letter, makes you feel about yourself:

God told Jeremiah, 'Up on your feet! Go to the potter's house. When you get there, I'll tell you what I have to say.'
So I went to the potter's house, and sure enough, the potter was there, working away at his wheel. Whenever the pot the potter was working on turned out badly, as sometimes happens when you are working with clay, the potter would simply start over and use the same clay to make another pot.
Then God's Message came to me: 'Can't I do just as this potter does, people of Israel?' God's Decree! 'Watch this potter. In the same way that this potter works his clay, I work on you, people of Israel. At any moment I may decide to pull up a people or a country by the roots and get rid of them. But if they repent of their wicked lives, I will think twice and start over with them. At another time I might decide to plant a people or country, but if they don't cooperate and won't listen to me, I will think again and give up on the plans I had for them.' (Jeremiah 18.1–12, Peterson, 1993)

Can you imagine this God moving over to make room for you?

This long-suffering God itching to obliterate is not the Being who lets-be. Sometimes the only sensible thing I can say about God is that God is paradox, but this is not paradox, it is cruel irony. A God who says 'If you are good and obey me, I shall be kind in return, but if you rebel I shall be angry and destroy you' is our waking nightmare. Faced with such a God, people either rebel or submit. They have no faith in this God, or too much faith in him.

Too much faith in a God who insists that he loves us even as he threatens us, seriously damages our ability to make free and responsible decisions. Rather than risk God's disfavour we will search the Scriptures for rules we can obey without the need for our own reflection. If God insists on holding us to account then we will insist on regulations to keep us on the straight and narrow path God has prescribed. In a communion of frightened people anyone straying outwith the boundaries of God's tolerance or deviating from accepted norms presents a danger to the rest. He or she (or they) must be brought into line or shunned for ever.

Shunning is not common practice in the Anglican Communion but a milder version of it allowed women with vocations for the priesthood to be ignored for centuries, and then compromised with flying bishops. No doubt 30 years from now women bishops will be firmly established – what was all the fuss about? In 50 years' time openly gay bishops may be as uncontroversial as female priests are now. For the Spirit is determined to blow away all our misconceptions about God, and none of the boundaries we find it necessary to hide behind will stand for ever between us and God's hope for us.

The trouble is that the idea of a God of boundaries is not wholly unattractive, especially to those of us who like to have some difficult decisions made for us rather than by us. The doctrine of predestination takes these boundaries to their limit by asserting that God's sovereignty gives God the right to choose some of us for salvation and leave the rest beyond the pale. Since we are all totally depraved anyway, neither the saved nor the damned can claim grounds for complaint.

Thankfully, the fact that God has the right to pre-ordain his creatures does not oblige him/her to do so. God whose love is expressed in letting-be is free to do what love requires. God chose to create not destroy, and God is creating still. We are a work in progress – not a completed creation, packaged and consigned to heaven or hell. As for the issue of our total depravity, we shall tackle this in the next chapter. There we will see that we are all falling short of our divine potential in the same way that a toddler can be expected to fall short of a PhD.

Meanwhile, God chooses me when he elects to create my unique and unrepeatable self, and God's love will not let him/her renege on that decision. This means that my own freedom is limited by God's first choice – I cannot decide *not* to be a creature – but this limitation turns out to be the key to real happiness. Freedom is not about the number of decisions we can make for ourselves to exert our independence. Freedom is knowing I am loved by the God who is wholly good and totally committed to letting-be me.

God is love and will do what is required to let creation be. While the passage from Jeremiah reminds us that, as Creator, God has unassailable rights, we know in our hearts that God cannot exert those rights in any way that contradicts love. God cannot hate. God cannot reject. A God who will go so far but no further in the enterprise of creation has no hope of seeing the commonwealth of love inaugurated. As we shall see in Chapter 3, love not law is the heart of the matter.

If you are finding this unsettling it could be that the God you have heard about and read about and sung hymns to for many years is more demanding than loving. Don't worry. Here is some advice from Anthony de Mello that may help:

We have been brought up to believe that God is a demanding God rather than a loving Father who loves us unconditionally. The best way to correct that notion is to stop measuring up to the demands, real or imaginary, that we think God is making on us. Do not give in to the demands of the beloved; give in only to the demands of the love in your own heart. If you ignore the love in your own heart and strive to give more than you have the love for, you will end up by either feeling guilty or resentful. Far from increasing your love, this will make it diminish. (de Mello, 1990)

## PAUSE AND REFLECT

Recently I was asked by a young woman who had become a Christian if she should leave her boyfriend who is an atheist in order to please God. In the light of de Mello's advice, what would you tell her about God that might illuminate her thinking? What is God demanding of you at the moment? Look for the things you feel you should be doing, or you ought as a Christian to be attending to, or that you really must take on board. Compare these with the things love is inviting you to choose. You may experience God as so demanding that there is no space in your life to hear this still, small voice of love. If this seems to be the case, you can be pretty sure that love is inviting you to stop measuring up to all those demands.

We are each on a quest to become our true, and therefore perfect, selves. On this quest we are helped by a God who moves over, and hindered by one who issues decrees. God the Father, Son and Spirit has faith in our quest and in us as we face life's trials. Faith is meant to be a friendship of equals where the responsibility for our life is all ours. While we make decisions for ourselves, and sometimes for the others in our company, God is the One who has initiated the quest and has made the only decision that really matters. Through everything that happens to us, God works to unite the whole of creation with him/her in a commonwealth of loving friendship.

This meeting of minds may be hard for us to imagine when we

look around us and at some of the decisions that humanity has made. Julian of Norwich believed that creation is like a nut held in the palm of God's hand. Our individual decisions are insignificant in the light of his/her decision to hold it there and nothing is impossible with love. 'Sin is necessary, but all will be well and all will be well, and all manner of things will be well', Mother Julian patiently insists (Mother Julian of Norwich, 1987 edn). She is not merely expressing her confidence in God. She is expressing God's confidence in his/her decision to create a commonwealth of free and responsible people. See what difference it makes to the way you think about yourself and your life when you let God tell you that, whatever is happening around you and to you at this time, all will be *well* and *all* will be well and all manner of things *will* be well.

You may discover that for all to be well a lot of things need to be different: not only the way we think about God and how we respond to God's decision to create, but also how we think about ourselves. Thinking differently is a decision we will make in the next chapter.

## References

de Mello, Anthony, SJ, *Contact with God*. India, Gujarat Sdahitya Prakash, 1990.

Heschel, Abraham Joshua, *Man Is Not Alone*. New York, Noonday Press, Farrar, Straus and Giroux, 1951.

Macquarrie, John, *Principles of Christian Theology*. London, SCM Press, 1966.

Mother Julian of Norwich, *Revelations of Divine Love*. London, Hodder & Stoughton Christian Classics, 1987.

Peterson, Eugene, *The Message*. Colorado, NavPress Publishing Group, 1993.

# 2

## *Nothing to Fear*

———◦◦◦———

*To repent is not to feel bad but to think differently.*
(Hauerwas, 1983)

I hope after reading Chapter 1, and perhaps trying out some of my suggestions, you are beginning to think differently about the freedom that God has given you to make choices. Thinking differently, especially about the really significant issues in life, is never easy because the customary takes less effort. When we think about ourselves or God it is easy to reinforce patterns of thought and belief that we have always held. These are like well-worn grooves within us, familiar if not always comfortable.

Stories can help us to think differently. They surprise us, and for a moment we jump out of our groove and see things from a new perspective. Here's a story from Anthony de Mello that I used to tell a friend of mine who suffered from Alzheimer's disease. He tended to worry about some decisions from his past and I was concerned to set his troubled mind at rest. Whenever these memories disturbed him I would remind him of the little girl who lived in a remote French village and claimed she talked to God, and that God talked back. The somewhat sceptical village priest decided to check this out, so he interviewed the child and suggested that the next time she was talking to God she ask him to tell her what the priest's unconfessed sin was. The priest had never told anyone of this secret sin, so there was no way the child could know it. The child agreed to do this and a few days later she returned. When the priest asked her if she had done what he requested, the child nodded. 'And what did God say when you asked what my unconfessed sin was?' asked the priest. 'He said he couldn't remember,' replied the child. Then the priest knew she had indeed talked with God. The story never failed to make my friend and me chuckle. We were both surprised and delighted each time we encountered this forgetful God.

Thinking differently about God leads us to experience God in a new way, and this in turn helps us to make more creative decisions. A real awareness of God moving over to make room for creation and for us, God as exuberant source and hospitable destination of our life, may make so much sense that it transforms the way you think about life overnight. Or it may take some time to become part of you. Try to be hospitable to the idea, move over, and give it room. Begin by looking at each day to discover where this exuberant God has been present and what he/she has been enthusiastically making room for. Are they the same things you have made a priority? Possibly not, but that is understandable. As well as thinking differently about God, we also need to find new ways of thinking about ourselves in relation to God. We need to repent.

Repentance is not possible without a degree of awareness. A dog can be trained not to chew table legs by the repeated application of reward and penalty, but it cannot be expected to become aware of the inappropriateness of destroying furniture. Its actions are controlled, but the dog does not repent of them. We, on the other hand, are very aware of ourselves. We know that we have an enormous capacity for self-deception, that we are capable of great wickedness, that even our purest intention has mixed motives. We constantly fall short of the goodness we know ourselves capable of, not because we fail to recognize the good, but because we refuse to do it. If we look at history, both ancient and modern, it seems that our response to God's loving act of creation has been extraordinary ingratitude. God moved over to make space, but we have fenced off space, defended our space, grabbed the space of others. What is wrong with us?

Not much really. God did not make any mistakes when he/she

created life and we have not fallen from grace. Death is not the punishment for sin but the biological price we pay for life. When we begin to think differently about God's decision to create we discover that sin is not a state of wickedness, to be judged forensically and punished in God's court of law. It is a very personal struggle between freedom and fear.

Before we explore that struggle it will be helpful to take a look at the story of Adam and Eve. This powerful tale can be either a stumbling block or a stepping stone on our quest to become our true and perfect selves. The choice is one of interpretation and the choice is ours. The story of Adam and Eve began life as a sobering tale told round ancient fires to explain the universal human experience of life as toil followed by death. Every generation that gathered around the fire knew from personal experience that life was hard. But why, they wondered, did it have to be that way and was there a time when things were different? The story of how things used to be endured and eventually appeared in Jewish Scripture. The Christian 'spin' on it came much later – the apportioning of blame made possible by understanding the story as real history rather than true myth. Christianity, not Judaism, decided that the fault was ours. The Garden of Eden became the theatre for a tale of sexual sin and punishment titled 'The Fall of Man'. The resultant theology of inherited guilt and a paradise lost has been around for a long time, influencing societies and controlling individuals through a system of reward and punishment that no dog trainer would sanction. Yet the power of the myth remains. It can help us understand ourselves by expressing that unease we all inherit not from ancestors in the Garden, but from our experience in the womb.

## PAUSE AND REFLECT

Birth was the expulsion from the paradise of an hospitable womb where all your needs were met even before you felt them, by a powerful muscle squeezing and pushing you towards a too small birth canal. What do you know about this experience? If your parents are still alive, let them tell you the tale once more. A very quick labour means that those contractions began strong and unremittingly. What would it have been like to find yourself suddenly plunged into this intensely physical vortex? Foetal heart monitors record an infant's distress, but they cannot tell us what she is thinking and feeling and how she is interpreting her fear. A long labour gives time for a growing unease and possibly a feeling of being trapped as the amniotic fluid seeps away and leaves the infant stranded. What happened in those vital seconds after the head is delivered and once the infant is born is part of the story too. Were you carefully wrapped and cuddled or did your condition mean that you were stretched out for examination and assaulted by tubes?

Whatever your experience, one thing is certain: none of it was your fault. But what if, like the ancients around the camp fire, this powerful experience left you uneasy: 'What have I done wrong to be so summarily cast out from paradise?' You may spend the rest of your life trying to run away from or deny the responsibility you suspect is yours. Your unease is unfounded, but this only makes it more difficult to shift – no matter how many snakes you point to or bushes you hide behind.

Life was always going to be difficult not because of some inherited fault, but because of our inherited freedom. While its conception and birth limits a dog to being a dog and a cat to being a cat, no such limitation-by-instinct exists for a human infant. While other animals are what they are and can never question the parameters of this existence, history testifies that each new *Homo sapiens* is challenged beyond mere survival and the passing on of genes. At birth we are the most helpless of all the animals. At one level this helplessness is a direct result of the narrowing of the female cervix that occurred when our distant ancestors began to walk upright. A narrow cervix necessitated an earlier birth of infants and these were less able to look after themselves. At another level this helplessness is really the gift of freedom. Somewhere between conception and birth, cats and dogs have hard-wired into them a set of instincts they cannot resist. We alone are not coerced by instincts. We are the creatures God chooses, but does not compel. We receive a mandate for more; a quest to become fully human. With each cry of protest against the limits of the way things are we accept the challenge and therefore the challenger.

This freedom from the absoluteness of instincts is a double-edged sword. Ignorance, after all, can be bliss. On the plus side, it liberates us from the limitations of our animal nature. However, we still face real dangers and experience real fears and these are made more acute by our lack of the fixed instinctual behaviour that is so quick and effective in other animals. Human existence could not have developed without freedom from the fixation of action by instincts, but this freedom, like a lively imagination, is an ambiguous gift. Interestingly, it has been observed that children nowadays are not totally independent of their parents until the age of 25. Not only is freedom an ambiguous gift, but children are too!

Of course, we all still have instincts and they operate all the time. Each child born has a powerful will to survive and a set of lungs to ensure that basic needs are brought to the attention of those who can meet them. Faced with danger, her adrenal gland will not fail to secrete hormones into the bloodstream. These prepare her body for one of two instinctual responses: fight or flight. However, she also has a brain that is in the process of developing and an identity that will be a work in progress even if she lives for 120 years. She can become aware of what makes her afraid and why – a crucial part of her journey into humanity.

Awareness of God who chooses, but does not compel, frees us from merely instinctual behaviour. Humanity is revealed as a relationship to God we can choose to grow into, or not. Other animals live to survive. They live in fear of extinction, compelled to pass on their genes. We have a choice. We can live in fear or we can live in love. The human story turns out to be a tale of love overcoming our instinct for flight or fight as God draws us away from the coercion of fear to the creativity of love.

In order to think differently about ourselves in relation to God we need to accept that love and fear are part of what it means to be a free human being. Both are necessary, and so is the tension between them in the same way that improvisation and order are intrinsic to art. The artist has a unique relationship with this tension, and from it produces his or her distinct work. In creation, God is the artist and 'a human being is a synthesis of the infinite and the finite, of the temporal and the eternal, of freedom and necessity, in short, a synthesis' (Kierkegaard, 1954).

God, wanting to let us be free, had to let us be afraid. This means that the relationship God has to us is one of complete understanding. God knows that we are both free and fearful. Some of our fear serves a purpose. It alerts us to real danger and awakens the fight or flight response to help us avert disaster. It informs us of our most basic needs – food, water, shelter, company – and we would be foolish to ignore such warnings. This is like the fear I have of dentists. I attend for regular check-ups because I am more afraid of the treatment I will need in the future if I do not look after my teeth in the present. This kind of fear is normal and useful; however, we were not created to serve our fears but to love our God. All of the violence and the lies that we call sin is our fight or flight response to a neurotic fear we have of the freedom to which God calls us.

Sin is therefore not a blemish to be ashamed of but a condition to be understood; an unease to be worked through one decision at a time. God is neither offended by nor afraid of our sin. Who could be offended by something as understandable as our fears? What has God to fear when even the worst of our actions will become immaterial in the fullness of time? I know that idea is shocking in a world where such wicked things are happening, and you may need some time to get used to it. I am saying that our sin does not matter to God (i.e. it does not affect God in the way that it affects us) because God understands what makes us afraid and why. The things we do, the decisions we make out of fear, will never be a part of God. In that sense they are immaterial. If we insist on making decisions that are immaterial to God we risk hearing those words of the bridegroom addressed to us: 'Truly, I say to you, I do not know you' (Matthew 25.12). After all, what is there to know? Too late we may discover that the death of the soul, while not a punishment, is nevertheless the inevitable consequence of letting fear drive us into the oblivion of non-being, one decision at a time. The God who lets-be is also the God who will let us go if that is what we choose.

When we understand the origins of sin not as a disgraceful fall from perfection, but as a state of anxiety about our ability to survive, we hopefully can feel a little of the compassion for our condition that God feels for us. After all, it is God who lets us be anxious. Wickedness is still wickedness, but to understand all is to forgive all and we need to forgive ourselves for all the poor decisions we have made in an attempt to fight our fears or fly from them before we can seek God's help to decide differently in the future. It will help to remember that love 'delights in the truth; it is always ready to excuse, to trust, to hope, and to endure whatever comes' (1 Corinthians 13.7, Jerusalem Bible). God's one action now as in the beginning is to let love flow, confident that whatever love creates will return to the lover who is prepared to endure because in the end 'perfect love casts out fear' (1 John 4.18).

None of this removes the responsibility each one of us has for our lives. It does, though, helpfully clarify that intrinsic to each decision we make is the choice between love and fear. Which of these shall we serve? This is the question Joshua put to the people of Israel:

Now therefore fear the LORD, and serve him in sincerity and in faithfulness; put away the gods which your fathers served beyond the River, and in Egypt, and serve the LORD. And if you be unwilling to serve the LORD, choose this day whom you will serve, whether the gods your fathers served in the region beyond the River, or the gods of the Amorites in whose land you dwell; but as for me and my house, we will serve the LORD. (Joshua 24.14–15)

Here is a story to which we can all relate: when Joshua told the Israelites to choose whom they would serve he was pointing out that we all serve someone or something. Service is intrinsic to creaturehood. But unlike other animals who must serve their instincts alone, we can choose whom or what we will serve. Joshua gives the people some possibilities: they could serve the gods of their ancestors, or the new gods of the people around them. They are free to choose, but choose they must; either consciously or unconsciously.

We too have choices. We can serve the patriarchal notions of God that our ancestors had. We can serve the New Age notions of God in contemporary society. We can serve the common weal or our individual well-being. We can serve the cause of love or we can continue as slaves to fear.

With one voice the people answered Joshua:

Far be it from us that we should forsake the LORD, to serve other gods; for it is the LORD our God who brought us and our fathers up from the land of Egypt, out of the house of bondage, and who did those great signs in our sight, and preserved us in all the way that we went, and among all the peoples through whom we passed; and the LORD drove out before us all the peoples, the Amorites who lived in the land; therefore we also will serve the LORD, for he is our God. (Joshua 24.16–18)

The people of Israel made a conscious decision to serve the Lord, yet many times they will renege on this decision, choosing to serve a different god or interest – sometimes consciously, often unconsciously. But here today they have declared their chosen intention and can be reminded of this moment of decision whenever it is necessary.

It is a good idea to consciously decide the direction we want our life to take. Those of us who never consciously choose one fundamental direction or another nevertheless choose by degrees. We are like explorers without a compass or a destination. We must wait until the end of all our days to discover where exactly we have arrived and whether or not we wanted to get there. The people of Israel declared their intention: 'as for my family and me, we will serve the Lord', and this decision was like a compass to help them whenever they lost their way.

The Eucharist serves the same purpose for the Christian Church. Each time we gather and place before ourselves the bread and the wine and the Word of welcome: 'Take, eat; this is my body' (Matthew 26.26), and of the wine: 'Drink of it, all of you; for this is my blood of the covenant, which is poured out for many for the forgiveness of sins' (Matthew 26.27–8), we look at where we have come and where we are going and, if need be, we re-align ourselves with our fundamental decision. The Eucharist is our compass.

Israel certainly had need of a compass, for in 2 Kings 17.5–8 and 13–15 (Jerusalem Bible) we read of the people forgetting the vow they made in the days of Joshua:

Then the king of Assyria invaded the whole country and, coming to Samaria, laid siege to it for three years. In the ninth year of Hoshea, the king of Assyria captured Samaria and deported the Israelites to Assyria. He settled them in Halah on the Habor, a river of Gozan, and in the cities of the Medes.

This happened because the Israelites had sinned against Yahweh their God who had brought them out of the land of Egypt, out of the grip of Pharaoh king of Egypt. They worshipped other gods, they followed the practices of the nations that Yahweh had dispossessed for them . . . And yet through all the prophets and all the seers, Yahweh had given Israel and Judah this warning, 'Turn from your wicked ways and keep my commandments and my laws in accordance with the entire Law I laid down for your fathers and delivered to them through my servants the prophets'. But they would not listen, they were more stubborn than their ancestors had been who had no faith in Yahweh their God. They despised his laws and the covenant he had made with their ancestors, and the warnings he had given them.

Isn't this our story too? We are offered a creative fellowship with God and we choose this for ourselves. Then we discover just how radically different our God of love is to all the 'other gods' we are used to serving. Each step we take towards God separates us from the crowd who are busy serving their fears. This can be a lonely experience. Rather than work through that sense of isolation that is a crucial part of any spiritual journey we are tempted to run back the way we came (Israel once wanted to return to Egypt), looking around us for the kind of slavery that masquerades as safety in numbers:

> We are in the minority in the great realm of being, and, with a genius for adjustment, we frequently seek to join the multitude. We are in the minority within our own nature, and in the agony and battle of passions we often choose to envy the beast. We behave as if the animal kingdom were our lost paradise, to which we are trying to return for moments of delight, believing that it is the animal state in which happiness consists. We have an endless craving to be like the beast, a nostalgic admiration for the animal within us. (Heschel, 1951)

This passage of Heschel's always comes to my mind when I consider the tide of reality television programmes now being broadcast. Many of them encourage us to be entertained by the misfortunes of others. Isn't this reminiscent of the gladiatorial ring? Even worse are those sad programmes that herd people together and encourage them to drink themselves senseless and play sex games with strangers in the pubs and clubs of holiday resorts. Such programmes promote the message that if we allow 'the animal within us' to control us, life will be fun and we will be happy. As though casual sex was ever a mark of humanity.

There are of course a variety of ways to 'join the multitude' and keep our clothes on. Those of us who join the Church may do so not to be in communion with God, but to be corralled by him with others who think the same way as we do. We want to be made good or kept safe by God's laws as though God were like the Pharaoh of Egypt administering a nation of slaves. Freedom is inseparable from human existence, but it is an awesome call – and one that we are quite prepared to turn a deaf ear to in many subtle and holy-looking ways.

Joshua's people choose to serve God in spite of the isolation from other nations this caused, because, as they looked back, they could see that God had kept faith with them throughout their journey. If we are to serve the cause of love until the establishment of the commonwealth, then we too need to know our reasons. We need to look back at our life so far and ask the question, 'Where has God been in my life and what has God been doing?'

## PAUSE AND REFLECT

Think back over the last 24 hours. Play the day like a video in your memory, beginning with when you woke. Picture as many scenes as you can and try to recall not only the action, but also your feelings. If you become distracted because a particular memory sets you off on a train of thought, then go back to the scene and simply notice what was going on there. Try not to judge what you remember (a sure sign that you are not yet thinking differently about the human condition we call 'sin'), but be hospitable to the whole lived experience, accepting every sensation, every emotion, every mood and action as part of your story. Then, when you have recalled as much of your day as you can, ponder these two questions. Where was I drawn by love? Where was I driven by my fears?

You see God is drawing us to complete union with him and this action is one continuous movement in our lives. To be drawn by God is to experience life as a series of invitations that flow into one another. We respond through the decisions we make and these become part of us. The decisions we make in turn make us. Those made in accordance with God's action set us free and fit us for the commonwealth. Those that resist God's action will not directly promote the kingdom, but God's mercy combined with an honest recognition of fear expressed in violence or lies can bring life out of the most deathly error of judgement.

This drawing action of God is an experience only human beings know. A salmon is not drawn to return to the river in which it was spawned and in which it will lay its own eggs. It is driven to return. Nothing but death will alter its course, and anyone who has watched the repeated efforts of scores of salmon to clamber over one another and over jagged rocks and through white water knows they have no choice in the matter. The salmon is not free to turn back. It cannot change its mind. Perhaps you know one or two people who spend their lives acting as though they were salmon.

To be *driven* through a day is very different from being *drawn*, yet most of us do not even notice when it happens to us. Driven people are stressed people and the evidence is all around us – road rage being a very good example. Our journey home is interrupted by roadworks, congestion and a less experienced driver who, being one interruption too many, becomes the target for our pent-up stress and frustration. Being driven means that we experience life not as a series of invitations, but as one demand after another, one interruption after another. At the root of all this stress and aggression lie fear and anxiety. Driven people are often anxious to please or frightened of disapproval. They are burdened by a sense of duty and resent this. Consequently, many situations can feel difficult; to be endured rather than lived. These never become an acknowledged part of us because we deny that they should have happened and refuse to integrate them into our story. Driven people are provoked into acts of violence or denial (fight or flight) as they try to defend themselves from their inner demons of fear.

I am sure as you look over your 24 hours again you will see that in any one day, even in any one action, we can be both driven and drawn. All of us are like Martha – driven by the need to be the good hostess, impatient with the interruption to her routine caused by Jesus and his friends' unexpected visit, and seeking approval for her chosen role. We are also like Mary – drawn to the words of Jesus and finding the courage to flout convention to take her place in the company of men around him. You have been both driven and drawn through the day, but you have not been alone. The God whose love overflows and who labours incessantly with the one goal of enjoying communion with a free creation was present in every instant of time and every fibre of this universe. Where has God been in your particular experience and what has God been doing?

One thing is certain. God has not been fastidiously picking his way through our sins and mistakes. We know because the life of Jesus demonstrates this; that God is not afraid to wade through the messy bits with us and for us. Think of Jesus in the midst of cursing fishermen and pungent fish. Think of him standing beside the women about to be stoned for adultery. Recall him stretching his hand towards a man rotting with leprosy. God is present in both the ordinary events of our routine and in the extreme highs and lows of life. Intent on drawing us to greater and greater freedom, God uses every situation to give us choice, always hopeful that we will choose love.

## PAUSE AND REFLECT

Place before yourself an image of God's love. It could be a picture of Christ on the cross. It could be a candle, a bowl of water and a towel, or bread and wine. It could be a photo of a newborn child or a breathtaking landscape. Whatever you choose, spend some time gazing at it before asking: 'What have I done for love? What am I doing for love now? And what ought I to be doing for the sake of love?' Do not be afraid to let the answers break your heart. God will restore it. For now, resolve to serve love and to encourage others to do the same.

Your review of the last 24 hours tells a tale that is shared by humanity as a whole. If we look back over history, piecing together as much of our human story as possible, we find that we have been driven by fear and drawn by love.

Fear tells us that we have needs that must be met. This, of course, is true; we all need food, water, shelter and community. There is often some truth at the root of even our most neurotic fear. Sadly, we have excused heinous acts of aggression and the capricious exploitation of man, beast and nature in order to meet our needs. The less authentic our need, the more determined we seem to secure it. Succeeding societies have made decisions that disregard the well-being of creation either by ignoring the ties between the present and the future, or between the individual and the universal. Cutting down the rainforests, hunting a species to extinction, polluting rivers and seas, were all decisions made by men and women like us, driven by fear that if our needs are not met we will not be alive, or happy or fulfilled. Not all our needs are authentic; we need food and water, shelter and clothes, but we don't need luxury foods or designer clothes. We need freedom to be ourselves, but we do not need the extremes of privacy that advertisers so successfully sell us.

Thankfully throughout history we have looked for a better way to live; have formed various ethics, according to time and culture, in our attempts to manage our needs with guiding principles for a good life. Questions about goodness, duty, values and conscience are as much part of our history as the pogroms and asylum detention centres we have felt the need for. Our persistent attempts to answer the question of how to live well, rather than the quality of those answers, are cause for hope and signs of God's Spirit. Yet it seems clear that while ethics, medieval or modern, religious or humanist, can point us to the good they cannot empower us to do it.

God has been in everything, every moment of history, every attempt to define and live the ethical life, every failure to follow the wisdom we are nevertheless able to comprehend. In all of it God has been doing only one thing: drawing humanity away from all our unhelpful fears to the unity with one another and with God that is freedom. Such kindness prompts in us a new response of gratitude and perfect trust. From this can flow a spontaneous and radical obedience to God's will in each moment of decision. That at least is what we see when we contemplate the life of Jesus and the decisions he made.

## References

Hauerwas, Stanley, *The Peaceable Kingdom*. Indiana, University of Notre Dame Press, 1983.

Heschel, Abraham Joshua, *Man Is Not Alone*. New York, Noonday Press, Farrar, Straus and Giroux, 1951.

Kierkegaard, Søren, *The Sickness Unto Death*. Princeton University Press, 1954.

# 3

# *Putting Faith into Action*

---

*Pray attentively and you will soon straighten out your thoughts.*

(Merton, 1973)

What is it that we are doing when we make a choice? I think we are putting our faith into action. How much faith and whether we act spontaneously or after careful thought depends on the significance of the decision. When we book a summer holiday we put some faith in our own taste and experience, or in the person who recommends to us the destination. We trust that our health and wealth will continue and that the holiday company, airline, hotel, etc. will function in a way that will support our choice. Without thinking too much about it we are expressing faith that the world will continue to spin and that the wars and natural catastrophes we read about in our newspapers will not affect us personally.

What a shock when our faith turns out to be misplaced. We are outraged when our hotel is only half-built or we suffer long delays on our journey due to industrial action. When our job becomes redundant or our pension scheme collapses, we are devastated. Should serious illness strike, robbing us of control over our own lives and decisions, we wonder what it has all been for.

Choosing is about putting faith into action, so it is important to know in what or in whom we put our faith. God put his/her faith in humanity by sending the Son to be one of us. We are invited to do the same. To have faith in Jesus is to believe that human love can overcome human fear. Jesus thought so, and God raised him from the dead to affirm this – 'If Christ has not been raised, your faith is futile and you are still in your sins' (1 Corinthians 15.17) – and to inaugurate in the risen Christ the commonwealth of love that will last for ever.

Christ is risen indeed. However, having faith that he was who he thought he was and has done something on my behalf that makes sense of my life, redeeming all my losses, is not the end of my salvation story, but only its beginning. This is why Jesus told some Jews who believed in him, 'If you continue in my word, you are truly my disciples, and you will know the truth, and the truth will make you free' (John 8.31–2). The truth is that when the risen Christ broke free from the tomb he also broke the trance of fear that holds humanity captive. This trance hides from us the possibility of the kingdom present in every cell of the universe. Knowing the truth is knowing what God knows and what Jesus proved – that love is more powerful than fear, more powerful even than death. Choosing to live in the kingdom of truth, waking up from our trance, requires not only faith *in* Jesus but the faith *of* Jesus. Readers familiar with the Spiritual Exercises of Ignatius will recognize this movement from belief to discipleship, as the gift the Spirit gives generously as we pray to know Jesus more through the contemplation of his life as it is recorded in the Gospels.

When I read the Gospels I encounter a man more interested in sharing his concerns for humanity than establishing his authority over it. He was happy to be part of that humanity, even refusing the hierarchical structures and honorific titles that his companions wished to bestow on him. Perhaps he recognized their attempt to make him the kind of Messiah who could be relied upon to absolve his followers of all responsibilities save childlike obedience of the patriarchal will. In Mark 8.29 when Peter confesses 'You are the Christ', Jesus 'gave them strict orders not to tell anyone about him' (Mark 8.30, Jerusalem Bible). He has no wish to be known as their Messiah, and instead deliberately embraces his humanity by referring to himself as the 'Son of Man'. It is now a reverential title, for we are as determined as the first disciples to define Christ to suit ourselves, but stripped of this piety it means the 'Human One'. This title first appears in Daniel's apocalyptic visions. There the Son of Man reassures Jews being persecuted that a higher justice would prevail. The higher justice that Jesus embodies is the power of God's love to overcome fear and its consequences in the world, not with imperial might but with human forgiveness, inclusiveness and service.

We need to think again (repent) if our belief in Jesus is really relief that here is someone offering us a religious or moral stronghold that will keep us safe from the world and our souls untouched by all the wrong choices we make and the selfish goals we tend to pursue. A fortress of certainty may look inviting in a chaotic world. Those of us who enter it, however, are obliged to leave our freedom, and therefore our humanity, at the gate. This can seem like a small price to pay, but it is not one we can afford. When we look to God to be some kind of benign dictator we inevitably discover that strongholds are exclusively inhabited by tyrants.

Saddam Hussein ruled Iraq with absolute terror. Anyone who refused to believe in him or tried to voice an opinion different from his was killed. His police committed atrocities under his orders, not daring to question their validity. God is not like Saddam Hussein, yet in his name Christians have been guilty of inhumane acts as large as the Crusades and as insidious as the persecution of homosexuals. They were all under orders.

I was struck by a radio broadcast from Iraq in the days just after the US army arrived in Baghdad. At the time people were looting every public building, and also some private ones, in the city. One man protested that the US army should do something to stop people exerting their freedom in this lawless way. 'Make us good,' he seemed to be insisting. The soldier, himself there under the orders of politicians, would certainly have been within his rights to reply that his job had been to make Iraq free from tyranny. It was for the people to make themselves good.

The life, death and resurrection of Jesus makes us free from the tyranny of our existential fear. We make ourselves good, that is, we grow into free and responsible human beings, not by having faith in Jesus – as a toddler has faith in loving parents that they will feed and clothe and keep her safe – but by exercising the faith of Jesus.

## PAUSE AND REFLECT

If faith is a journey from 'faith in Jesus', to 'the faith of Jesus', where are you on the road between these two? Hint: at the start of this journey (and some of us stay here our whole lives) we look for very clear guidance about every detail of human life. If we cannot have instincts to control us and relieve us of the responsibility for our decisions, we will take regulations. Who better to give them than the Son of God? Those who are putting their faith into action want to get to know Jesus the man; not just what he said and did, but what motivated him. They pray for the grace 'to know Jesus intimately, to love him more intensely, and so to follow him more closely' (Ignatius, Spiritual Exercises, quoted in Fleming, 1980).

It would be useful at this point to read through the Gospel of Mark, paying particular attention to decisions that Jesus took. A climatic point is of course his decision to go to Jerusalem, but it is worthwhile noticing the number of decisions Jesus makes before this one. In Mark 1 alone you will read that he decides to go to John for baptism and leaves Nazareth to do this. He decides to go into the desert for a while, after which he chooses to go to Galilee. There he decides to begin a preaching ministry and makes this a priority: 'And he said to them, "Let us go on to the next towns, that I may preach there also; for that is why I came out"' (Mark 1.38). He invites some fishermen to be his companions. If you spend time contemplating each decision that Jesus took to put his faith into action, you will begin to notice that what he said and what he did were expressions of who he was. He taught the kingdom and he demonstrated the kingdom because he is the kingdom. Jesus is the man who discovered that love is more powerful than fear; that God's decision to create matters more than any of our decisions to destroy; that mercy, and not might, holds the key to the commonwealth of peace.

By the end of that first chapter of Mark's Gospel Jesus has chosen to heal a man suffering from leprosy, has taught in the synagogue, and decided to keep his identity a secret. He has also made space for private prayer.

Prayer for Jesus was not thinking through the arguments for each choice. Remember that when we think we tend to reinforce patterns of thought and belief that we have always held. These are like well-worn grooves within us. We read the books and newspapers that agree with our theology or our politics. We have to make a conscious decision to do otherwise, perhaps because we are studying and need to be informed by both sides of an argument before we conclude that our way of thinking was the right one.

Prayer is different. It is an open-ness to all the possibilities that God created when God created this diversity we call the universe. Prayer is a question with as many answers as there are stars in the sky. When we pray, we jump out of the groove to ask God and ourselves 'What if?'

What if God never learned to read a map and therefore cannot recognize one nation state from another? Think of all the prayers we offer for our particular country: its people, government, climate, economy. It makes sense to us to pray separately for those who are near us and those who are far off, but from God's perspective we are all close up and connected both to him and to one another. What if God, not having a map with which to locate the boundaries of our petitions, answers our prayers on a global scale? During the recent BSE outbreak in Britain many churches and many individual Christians prayed for the farmers and their families. What if God understood our prayers to be for farmers everywhere – not just those in Britain, and not just those affected by this particular disaster?

What if we took God seriously when God says 'For my thoughts are not your thoughts, neither are your ways my ways' (Isaiah 55.8)? Imagine some of the world's problems: famine, an AIDS epidemic, terrorism. Now imagine the Holy Spirit like an eagle soaring high above these problems. What do they look like from that distance? Next imagine the Holy Spirit like that sharp sword 'piercing to the division of soul and spirit, of joints and marrow, and discerning the thoughts and intentions of the heart' (Hebrews 4.12). What do the world's problems feel like from this probing proximity? Consider all the difficulties the politicians cite about climate, Third World debt, corruption, military juntas, etc. as reasons why we cannot simply give food to hungry people, even though we have a surfeit of food in the world. Does the Holy Spirit see these difficulties from her perspective? Does she nod understandingly at their insurmountable nature?

I don't think so. The root cause of famine is fear. All wars are caused by fear; God knows this. We are afraid to share our wealth in any meaningful way so we lie and fight to keep what we have and pretend to ourselves that this makes us happy. Our fear keeps millions hungry. It gives birth to the violence of terrorism and the lies of hypocrisy. We see this writ large in international politics, but violence and lies are also very much a part of the domestic scene. The fear that sells arms to support a dictator, then goes to war to remove that same dictator, is not so very different from the fear that tolerates incarceration for asylum seekers or refuses to 'let-be' those of a different religion, culture or sexuality in our street.

Try the 'What if?' approach to prayer for yourself and you will discover, as Jesus did, that prayer is different and a whole lot more dangerous than sitting thinking quietly about things you've thought about before. It is not listening *to* God tell us what we should believe, think, do. A friend of mine once observed, 'God never tells me what to do or where to go. God invites me to choose.' Quite right; God has no voice either inside me or external to me with which to 'speak'. We need to be careful, I think, when we say things like 'God told me' this or that, especially if God told us something about someone else or about what the Church should or should not be doing. This kind of thing is usually wishful thinking. We want to be sure more than we want to be free. When I am very sure about what God is communicating over and above the certainty that God is at all times communicating love, then I am probably misled by my own prejudices and peccadilloes. As we will see, this sometimes leads us to make decisions that look very holy or good but which don't turn out that way. For now we note that prayer is not listening to a voice that is just as likely to be the voice of my conscience or my prejudice or my inclination, as that of God. Prayer is being aware *of* God creatively present in every cell of the universe. It is letting God be in all things.

## PAUSE AND REFLECT

Consider the humility of God who does not insist on being recognized in creation but waits for his/her creatures, for us, to let God be in our day and in our community and in our lives. Each time you come to prayer remind yourself that God waits for you to let him/her be. What response do you feel yourself wanting to make to this gracious God?

The practicalities of prayer are much the same as those that apply in human relations. Sometimes my children come home from school to find me typing away on my word processor. They begin to tell me about their day and I make appropriate sounds as I continue to type. Then one might say, 'No, Mum, you've *really* got to listen to this.' The wise child knows a good story and does not want me to miss any part of it. So I have to stop what I am doing and demonstrate by my body language that I am giving my whole attention to what the child is telling me.

We become aware of God's presence and possibilities by being attentive. That means, just as it did for Jesus, going off by ourselves to a place with minimal chance of interruption at a time of the day when we are not likely to fall asleep. We pray by turning up for prayer so it is worth becoming aware of what space we give to our relationship with God at the moment so that we can decide if it is working or not. Are we thinking or praying? How much attention are we paying? Paul speaks about looking in the mirror, seeing the truth, and then turning away and forgetting what we have seen. To prevent this happening many people find it useful to take a note of what happens when they pray and this can be particularly useful in a time of decision. The journal is like a bookmark. It 'keeps our place' in the ongoing story of our relationship with God, so we know where to return the next time we pray. Being attentive often means being persistent; digging away at some area of our lives where God is labouring to reveal to us some new possibility. The journal records our excavations and the treasure we find.

To help us God is generously delighted to work with whatever time and attention we give to our relationship with him/her. We help ourselves if we identify and ring-fence in our busy week one or two, or three, spaces of about 45–60 minutes in duration for focused prayer and by turning up for these. Even then, God cannot make us pray if we want to think.

If Jesus had thought about it he probably would have remained a carpenter in Nazareth like his father and possibly his father before that. If he had thought about it, as Peter begged him to, he certainly would not have gone to Jerusalem during Passover. Travelling, teaching, healing, heading for Jerusalem; these choices are particular to Jesus of Nazareth but they came out of his prayer. We have our own decisions to make, but prayer is the only tool that will help us make them in partnership with God's intention for this world. It is the place where our faith in a God personally involved with creation meets our joys and sorrows, our doubts and dogmas, and the necessity for action. It is where God warmly invites us to choose.

For each decision Jesus makes ask yourself: 'Where is love in this and where is fear?' You will find that Jesus always lived the life of love. He preached the kingdom and demonstrated it by showing love that was inclusive, love that forgave, love that served. It was a manifesto for peace that discomforted many.

Take, for example, the argument about divorce. The Pharisees asked Jesus to comment on the legal grounds by which a man could divorce his wife. They knew there was more than one school of thought on the matter. We read in Mark 10.1–12 that he ignores their quibbles about the legal niceties and tackles instead the issue of male power. He speaks against the inequality that allows a man to divorce a wife, but does not allow a woman to divorce her husband. First reminding the Pharisees of the Scripture – 'But from the beginning of creation, "God made them male and female." "For this reason a man shall leave his father and mother and be joined to his wife, and the two shall become one flesh." So they are no longer two but one flesh. What therefore God has joined together, let not man put asunder' (Mark 10.6–9) – he then drops the bombshell: patriarchy, not divorce, is the instrument of division he has in mind. It is patriarchy that violently divides a woman and a man, making one the property of the other though both are created equal by God.

Patriarchy is male power exerted aggressively over females and children. It probably developed when our ancestors gave up the nomadic existence of hunter gatherers and began to farm and build and gradually to own property. Property passed from father to son and power was needed to control the fertility of women to safeguard against a cuckoo in the nest. Women who had been equal partners in the struggle for survival became property too, and were denied their basic human rights. This situation still prevails in some cultures to this day and bubbles under the surface of many others where patriarchy is violence and lies dressed up as politics, theology and economics. It continues to exclude many by reserving power to a privileged few, even in democracies.

The kingdom points out abuse of power and includes everyone

as it pursues non-violent ways to resist the aggression of the elite and of the bully. This requires courage, emotional maturity and spiritual awareness, like that shown by Gandhi when he persuaded the British to quit India, or by the African National Congress in the early 1980s when it began to think differently about its struggle against apartheid and embraced non-violent means to end the apartheid government. 'For he that is not against us is for us' (Mark 9.40).

## PAUSE AND REFLECT

Where in both the public and private areas of your life do you act for God's inclusive commonwealth, and where do you collude with those who stand against it? Even deciding to tell a joke can be an act of violence against someone. Freud recognized that humour is masked aggression, and women have been the subject of enough humour to know this is true. But are women now fighting back with the same kind of aggression?

Even before the discussion about patriarchy Jesus had made powerful enemies. In Mark 3 we read that Jesus in the synagogue encountered a man with a withered hand: 'And they were watching him to see if he would cure him on the sabbath day, hoping for something to use against him' (Mark 3.2, Jerusalem Bible). Surely Jesus knew this, for he said to the man: 'Stand up out in the middle!' (Mark 3.3, Jerusalem Bible.) No quiet healing in a corner then, but instead he turned to his detractors: 'Is it against the law on the sabbath day to do good, or to do evil; to save life, or to kill?' (Mark 3.4, Jerusalem Bible). His challenge was greeted with truculent silence. 'Then, grieved to find them so obstinate, he looked angrily round at them, and said to the man, "Stretch out your hand". He stretched it out and his hand was better. The Pharisees went out and at once began to plot with the

Herodians against him, discussing how to destroy him' (Mark 3.5–6, Jerusalem Bible).

The kingdom serves through acts of compassion and chooses the good over the expedient. Recently the Episcopal Church in Scotland decided, in principle, that the time has come to allow the Holy Spirit to call a woman priest to the office of bishop. Five years previously the call of women to the priesthood by the same Spirit had been recognized and made room for in that community. The delay illustrates the struggle we all have, to choose the good over the expedient when doing so may bring us into conflict with others who see things differently or wield a power we would prefer to placate. Glass ceilings and no-go areas may seem to keep the peace. Too often we use them to shield us from the hard work of pursuing justice – the foundation of true peace and compassion. No doubt this work was going on beneath the glass ceiling of the Scottish Episcopal Church and away from the glare of the media. Yet the decision to restrict the call of women, however temporary and expedient, robbed all women, and not just those with vocations to the priesthood, of their dignity in a way difficult to imagine Jesus commending.

## PAUSE AND REFLECT

What role does expediency play in your life? When have you faced, as Jesus did on that sabbath day, the choice between the expedient response to God's love and the courageous one? What helped you and what hindered you in your decision, and how do you feel about your choice now?

Again and again his enemies sought to trap Jesus into speaking or acting against the Law so that they could get rid of him. He could have prevaricated or responded with formulaic answers, but Jesus chose to live dangerously; refusing to lie in order to flee from his enemies. Expediency can be another term for fear, which is why Jesus did not choose to serve it. He knew that we have nothing to fear.

Later in the Garden of Gethsemane he chose to acquiesce to a loss of control over his own life, even to lose it, in order to keep faith with the Father. Loss of control is not something too many of us choose for ourselves. We go to great lengths and considerable expense to insure against the kind of chance that threatens to take away our control and we take it very hard when this does not make us immune to the situations of loss that can happen in any life. Jesus in the Garden demonstrates that living securely (even if it's more than an illusion) is not the same as living in fellowship with God. The kingdom is not a place full of strong and powerful people, but those who chose love over fear, God's hope over our despair. 'I am the way, and the truth, and the life' (John 14.6), Jesus said as he demonstrated faithfulness to God and self-giving love to the community as the only life worth living, and one even worth dying for.

There are situations of loss in every life that invite our acquiescence. These include loss of a loved one, loss of employment, loss of a vision, loss of health or youthfulness. It may not feel as though we have much choice in these matters. They seem to overtake us and the accompanying loss of control over our own lives terrifies us. Jesus' acquiescence to this loss of control, his acceptance of his own arrest, torture, trial and horrendous death, does suggest a choice; to live not in control of our own lives, but faithful to our relationship with God and to God's way in the world.

For it turns out that God's way is to bring life out of death. Just as we are liberated by a God who moves over to make room for us, so we are freed from our slavery to fear by a God whom death (our ultimate fear) cannot hold. If I have nothing to fear but fear itself, then faced with a decision between what is the loving thing to do and what will keep me in control and what is mine safe, I may choose love. And with God's help, trust all my fears of loss to him/her. Making decisions on this basis – that God chooses to bring life from death as a way of redeeming us from our fears –

will turn the world upside down. This appears to be the essence of Jesus' faith and we are inaugurated into his death and resurrection when we begin to live this faith of his.

Not all of us will be called to stand, row on row, like Gandhi's followers and be beaten down as they were for the sake of this transformation. But we may be called to cry 'Enough is enough!' like the Zapatistas of Mexico who, in 1994, began a movement of those discontented with 'the good life' they were being sold by the market. They asserted their right to choose dignity, humanity, life and a new kind of democracy that saw through the myth of development and placed the economy at the margin of community and people at its centre. This kind of death is one we all need to embrace 'For what does it profit a man, to gain the whole world and lose his soul?' (Mark 8.36).

When we seek to know Jesus intimately we discover, as he did before us, that love overcomes fear when we make decisions for inclusiveness, for service and for the ongoing relationship with the Father. This led him increasingly to include all people in his mission when tradition demanded he ignore women, children and Gentiles. It drew him to serve rather than dominate, and he taught his disciples to serve one another when he washed their feet. When his enemies came for him he decided to give away control over his own life rather than save it. He could do this because he had discovered the significance of human life. Jesus understood what God had in mind when he/she moved over to create. In the Garden he adopted this purpose as his own. Hanging on the cross he did what he had always seen the Father doing: he forgave us our sins and so redeemed us from all the fears that prevent us from recognizing that God's purpose is in fact ours too; part of our nature. Now he invites us to follow him in a fellowship of human ones who, with our own lives, may advance the kingdom of God that his life has established.

# References

Fleming, David L., *The Spiritual Exercises of Saint Ignatius – A Literal Translation & A Contemporary Reading.* St Louis, Institute of Jesuit Sources, 3700 West Pine Boulevard, 1980.

Merton, Thomas, *The Wisdom of the Desert.* London, Sheldon Press, 1973.

# 4

## Digging for Discernment

*In making a choice or in coming to a decision, only one thing
is really important – to seek and to find what God calls me to
at this time of my life. I know that his call remains faithful; he
has created me for himself and my salvation is found in that
love. All my choices, then, must be consistent with this given
direction of my life.*

(Fleming, 1980)

When Ignatius of Loyola, a nobleman and soldier who lived in
sixteenth-century Spain, was in the first flush of his Christian
faith he encountered a lone donkey on a road. Ignatius had been
pondering which of two forks in the road he should take. He
decided to let the donkey decide. Whichever road the donkey
took, Ignatius would accept as God's will for him and take it also.
It was not an auspicious beginning, but later Ignatius developed
a prayerful process for discerning God's will in a time of decision
that was to prove helpful to people of faith in every century since.
No one knows what happened to the donkey.

Jesus intrigued his companions because he was often going off
by himself to pray. No doubt they made the connection between
these absences of his and the decisions he made when he
returned. Finding themselves increasingly attracted to the things
he said about life and the love he demonstrated, they asked him
to teach them to pray. Jesus replied with the following:

Our Father in heaven,
may your name be held holy,
your kingdom come,
your will be done,
on earth as in heaven.
Give us today our daily bread.
And forgive us our debts,
as we have forgiven those who are in
    debt to us.
And do not put us to the test,
But save us from the evil one.
        (Matthew 6.9–13, Jerusalem Bible)

It is a short prayer, well known to many who have been taught to memorize it in school. It carries in its simple petitions the tools for discernment handed down from one generation to another if only we knew how to handle them. Discernment is an excavation we carefully carry out in the ground of our will so that we can uncover the will (or hope) of God for us in the soil. This prayer is all we need to guide our discernment in times of choice, that's why Jesus recommends it to us.

## Our Father in heaven

Jesus invites us to notice what kind of 'Father' we are attending to with our prayer. Christian discernment is only possible if we begin from the premise that God is the kind of 'Father in heaven' who loves us before, during and after we choose, regardless of what we choose. God is not administering a reward scheme. He/she does not love us more if we make all the right moves. The Israelites discovered this when they chose to go into the desert rather than cross the Jordan river into the land God promised them. It was not a great choice, but God loved them, went with them, and took care of them. Then God brought them in due course back to the decision about that river. This time round they trusted their experience of God just enough to go forward into the land promised to them.

God never gives up on us because there is no limit to God and therefore to God's love. God is infinite and enjoys an infinity of possibilities. He/she does not have to insist on a particular choice for us. There was a time when Christianity saw it as a duty to terrorize people into the faith, especially those of different cultures who had a faith of their own. There was one door leading to the soul's salvation and everyone had to go through it. If they would not go willingly, then their bodies were killed in order that their souls might be saved. It is an extreme example from the history of religion, but we are still busy creating a God who is as limited as we are. If God is without limit, he/she cannot be snookered by our choices and is not anxious about them either.

## PAUSE AND REFLECT

Recall a time when you felt as though God had given up on you. Who in your life did God remind you of at that point? Spend some time recalling the situation and try to imagine Jesus present. Where is he? What is he doing? What is he saying? What is Jesus hoping you will notice about the nature of the Father's love?

God loves us unreservedly and is not thwarted by any choice we make, in the task of drawing us home. It is of course possible for a person to resist God. If we do this often enough it will become a habit, an attitude hard-wired into our souls. However, even for the most hardened soul, rejection of God as our heavenly Father remains to be ratified at some point in the future when our imperfect knowledge has ended: 'For now we see in a mirror dimly, but then face to face. Now I know in part; then I shall understand fully, even as I have been fully understood' (1 Corinthians 13.12).

Meanwhile, it is useful to remember that God does not have a blueprint of your life. Sometimes I wish God had a plan for me; life, I think, would be easier if I could peep at this blueprint, see precisely where I am meant to go, and know what God expects of me. But if God has a plan, then clearly this is kept hidden. My life would be an attempt to discover where God is hiding the plan, and this makes for a churlish deity. Why not just show me the plan as soon as I ask for it?

Discernment would not be necessary if God had a plan and was willing to show it to me. There would be no choices to make beyond the fundamental choice put to the Israelites by Joshua. Discernment is necessary because God has no plan; never had a plan. God has a desire, the capacity to fulfil that desire, and the will to do it. God desires unity with human beings who are fully alive, fully ourselves, and therefore fully able to reciprocate God's enjoyment of us and of creation. And there is no map to lead me to this freedom, only God's desire, like a magnet, and my awareness of the pull of God's longing on my life.

Paradoxically God cannot help but know what the best choice is for us in any circumstance. Though God does not choose to meet and save us in only one path (choice) to the exclusion of all others, God can prefer the one that will take me most directly to my goal.


## May your name be held holy

In any decision the first thing to do is identify our goal so that we do not confuse means and ends. To hold God's name as holy is a fundamental decision about the direction of my life and each time we pray it we remind ourselves that it is ours. As creatures, the only appropriate destination for us is God, who is at the centre of all life. But it is not the only option open to us. We are free to choose other directions for our lives. I could decide that 'fame' is my goal. Celebrity status is one form of this, but there are other kinds of fame and other degrees of it. I might want to be a famous maverick among my peers. If I am religious I might want to have a famous faith among my fellowship or in my denomination. I might even want to be a famous maverick of the faith! It's worth noting that we cannot enjoy acclaim and at the same time proclaim the holiness of God; either God is great or we are.

Probably the most famous person ever to live was Jesus. Yet Jesus did not choose fame, tempting though the prospect was for him when he thought about it in the desert. When the wealthy young man called him 'good', Jesus corrected him: 'Why do you call me good? No one is good but God alone' (Mark 10.18). God alone was Jesus' goal, unity with the Father's will his only consideration; a single-mindedness that made him an uncomfortable companion and a loose cannon to the establishment.

To keep God's name holy we must 'seek and to find what God calls me to at this time of my life'. Nothing else will do. This may seem obvious, but it is easily forgotten. With hardly any effort at all we can overlook God's priority in our life so that only once we have satisfied our own desire for wealth or power or a family do we remember to seek God in the life we have chosen for ourselves. This is decision-making by tick-tack-toe. The choices we make without reference to God are the lines drawn without much thought between dots. The relationship between one choice and another is seen later when we are 'boxed in' to a much more significant choice by our earlier carelessness.

## PAUSE AND REFLECT

Probably most of us over the age of 21 have already made some important decisions in our life with scant attention to our goal. It will be good to acknowledge this now and resolve to keep God's name and reputation holy by cultivating an attitude towards prayer and discernment that makes God's call our supreme concern. This resolve needs to be reviewed regularly and not just in a time of decision.

Look back and notice the choices you have made in the routine of life this week. What do they say about the direction you want your life to take? How satisfied are you that the choices you have made express the person you want to be? We look back in order to go forward more confidently. So decide what help you need in the coming week and ask God for this. Strengthen your resolve by praying that everything you do, every thought you have and everything that goes on inside you, might, by the grace of God, reflect your intention to live in communion with God.

Change may be called for or the renewal of some commitments we have already made. God works with all our decisions, even those we made for spurious reasons. The story of Israel's long relationship with God clearly demonstrates that God has a bias against change. We ignore this at our peril and because of our arrogance. There is so much in life that we can now change at will that we easily convince ourselves that all our problems will be solved with a new job or house or partner or religion. The faith of Jesus, expressed in this prayer, declares that all our decisions, past and present, can be forgiven, included in God's creative work and put to the service of God's commonwealth when we keep pressing towards our goal.

## Your kingdom come, your will be done

This could be the mantra of discernment. Even when we know our goal we still find it difficult to be wholly available to God's preferred choice in a concrete situation. When Jesus recommended that his friends pray for the kingdom to come, I think he was aware of how much help we need to keep God's options for us open long enough to grasp their potential – or at least gasp at their radical direction. Too often we, like the Pharisees, do not even glimpse the possibilities in a decision because we stand behind a wall of our own preconceptions with our fingers in our ears and our eyes tightly shut.

After the destruction on 11 September 2001 of the World Trade Center in New York by hijacked aeroplanes, commentators began to suggest that the USA's foreign policy was beginning to reap what it had sown. How far this is true is not the argument of this book, but the question it raises is. Soon after the USA suffered the biggest ever terrorist attack on its own soil, it declared a war on terrorism and told the world that those who would not join her in this struggle would be considered part of the terrorist community. What a pity, many observed, that in the struggle against global warming and pollution, when the international community called for solidarity, this same US government chose to shrug shoulders and walk away. But what if it hadn't done this? I wonder if we have really considered the ramifications of a superpower changing its mind about both domestic and foreign policy. Decisions made by the US government actually affect every citizen in the world more than their own governments do. If God's will for the world was a radical change of the foreign policy of the USA, this could have so many ramifications for those of us in the Northern Hemisphere that few of us are likely to pray for it.

Even in our own lives, when we pray 'Your kingdom come, your will be done' we may not really mean 'Show me your will and I will do it'. Few of us are that available to God. What we really mean is 'Show me your will and I'll do it if it accords with mine'. This attitude invalidates the discernment process. We attempt to discern because we believe that not only does God know what is the best among several good options, but we can know it too. Knowing brings its own responsibility. I have commented before that the difficulty we have is not knowing what decision to make, but actually taking it. Before we engage in a process of discernment we need to be clear that we will follow through to the point of action. Not to do so is to play with prayer and with God. 'Show me your will and I will do it' is prayer. 'Show me your will and I will think about it' is pride, the opposite of humility. It is to declare ourselves independent of God and of God's preferred will for our lives.

Most of us experience a special kind of resistance to this resolve. When it comes to the point of action we drag our feet. I am reminded of a walk I once took up a fair-sized hill. I knew that the view from the top would be spectacular and I very much wanted to see it. But about two-thirds of the way up I began to wonder if it could really be that good. It would be easier to go back down than struggle up those last few, steep metres. It took a renewed effort to keep going and eventually I was able to throw myself down on the grass at the summit, catch my breath, and then marvel at the countryside spread out before me.

If I had not kept going I would not have seen any of it. Praying to know God's will is the first two-thirds of a hill. Doing God's will, as it is revealed to us, is that last steep bit without which the rest is a waste of time and energy. There is in each of us a spirit of fear that does not want us to move into the kind of action that actually brings in the kingdom. The closer we get to a good decision the more strenuous the effort to make it becomes.

Next time you decide to give a decision prayerful consideration try praying to be wholly available to whatever would benefit God's commonwealth. If we have our goal clearly in sight, then there are many instrumental decisions we all are free to make. These are all means to our end. To marry or not, this occupation or that, how to serve the community, how to spend leisure time, how to respond to friends, family, disaster, hurts, not always being appreciated, etc.; these are all instrumental and are the kinds of decision we will want to consider prayerfully.

In order to be available we often need to gather some information about our options. It is useful to list this in columns, depending on whether it inclines us to accept a particular choice or reject it. For example, say I am offered promotion at work that will involve a move to another city. Clearly, there are things I need to know. My choice is between two options: accept the promotion or refuse it. In order to explore the question thoroughly I would head a sheet of paper with four columns:

| *Promotion* | *Promotion* | *Status quo* | *Status quo* |
| – *accept* | – *reject* | – *accept* | – *reject* |

If you have never tried this, or if you have done something similar but with only two columns – 'Promotion – accept' or 'Promotion – reject' – you will be surprised how useful those extra two columns can be. As I gather information, facts and figures, pros and cons, I enter these under the appropriate column. It is important at this point to be as hospitable as I can be to the whole of my self. If I am only committing my holy thoughts to paper and ignoring what appears to me to be my more selfish aspirations, the exercise will be flawed. Remembering that God is not afraid of our sins gives us the courage to excavate our motives truthfully. So if an increase in salary is attractive, this is entered in the 'Promotion – accept' column. This may further prompt me to enter under 'Status quo – reject' the fact that I am struggling on my present wage. These are two sides of the same coin, but the double entry helps bring to light the real hopes and fears of my life. These feelings are what I am discerning and the only way I know of being hospitable to them is to acknowledge them both on paper and in prayer. In prayer the Spirit of truth asks 'What if?', gently examining my feelings from all angles and uncovering the heart of the matter as an archaeologist patiently brushes centuries of dust off ancient bones that have a story to tell.

A reason for accepting the status quo may be my contentment with the friends I have in this city. One reason for accepting the *promotion* might be the desire to please my parents (even if they are no longer alive to see my success). It will take some time to uncover all that moves me on the one hand to accept, and on the other to reject, this change in my circumstances, and the time given needs to be proportionate to the significance of the decision.

Once the columns are exhausted I need to remind myself of the fundamental direction of my life because it is easy to lose sight of it in all the inspiration and perspiration of discovery. I probably need to pray again that God show me what the creative choice is for my life at this time and resolve that I will put this into action.

Then I look over my columns and begin to notice that some entries are more significant to my fundamental decision than others. Perhaps as a reason for keeping things the way they are, I have noted an uneasy feeling that career progress to date has been more luck than talent. The significance of this depends on how true it is. If it is an honest appraisal of my ability, then it might be quite weighty, but if it is a sign of low self-esteem this needs to be recognized without allowing it to greatly influence this current decision. The question to ask is always 'Where is love and where is fear?'

The considerations that hold more weight in the light of the gospel of Christ are the ones that, taken together, will point me, tentatively, to whichever alternative is the more reasonable; the more likely to be God's will for me. Objectivity can help at this point, so I might imagine what advice I would give to someone I do not know but who has made it clear to me that God's enterprise is their supreme concern. Or I could ask myself which decision I hope to be remembering on my death bed since this cuts through the distractions that obscure my fundamental values.

What! I hear you gasp; all this effort and we end up with a *tentative* decision? What happened to certainty? Certainty, like strongholds and blueprints, are not what discernment is about. Choosing is putting faith into action. Discernment is necessary because God has no plan and does not tell us where to go and what to do. God is the one inviting us to choose. Having come to my tentative decision it is therefore time to pray again. I offer my tentative choice to God as the way ahead most material to God's creative purpose and I ask God to confirm this. This too takes time. What we are doing is living with our decision as though it were final, but without putting it into action. We are seeing how it sits with us. Now it may sit quite uncomfortably, but still be the will of God. Or it may feel very comfortable but not be the will of God. It all depends on where these experiences of comfort and discomfort originate within us.

These different experiences come from a spirit of love or a spirit of fear and we need to discern the differences between them. Discernment of spirits is the art of noticing differences. In the material world we are all skilled at noticing differences; we are all discerning consumers. Imagine you are shopping for a man's lounge suit, either for yourself or for a reluctant male shopper in your life. You spot two suits in a shop window; both look attractive, so you enter. Approaching the suits you inspect each one closely with your hands and eyes. One suit holds up to this close inspection. The material feels hard-wearing. The stitches are true and the lining strong and generous. This suit will deliver what it promises; will keep its good looks for years and serve its wearer well. The second suit looks as good, though the feel of the cloth perhaps suggests a poorer quality, the stitches are careless in a few telling places, and the lining a little perfunctory. Over time this suit will begin to shine and become seated. Worse still, it may fall apart at the seams. You notice the differences and can make a decision based on your observations and presumably your bank balance too.

Christian discernment is simply noticing the difference that making room for God's commonwealth of peace brings to the way we live. Think of Jesus in the Garden of Gethsemane. Would he choose to save his life or lose it? He chose to lose it. It was a most uncomfortable decision – one from which every cell of his body must have shrunk. It was also the decision that gave him most peace, a deep-down sense of being at one with God, of being the right person in the right place at the right time.

When we discern we notice differences, sometimes quite small ones in the quality of our spiritual experience and our emotional lives. Noticing these differences takes some time and is a skill that needs to be developed through practice. We are complex characters and we are expert at deceiving ourselves. God coming close can cause me to feel happy but so can a slice of hot fudge cake. Gossip can excite me as much as the still small voice of the Holy Spirit can. Revenge can taste as good as the Eucharist, especially when we pretend righteousness to hide the violence of our emotions. Judas probably convinced himself that he was being brave and good when he lied to Jesus and the disciples and sold his master for a few coins to save his own skin. We are all a bit like Judas and it takes some courage to discern the lies and violence operating within us because we are reluctant to have these exposed, even to our own selves.

When I pray about a decision, not every thought, insight, image or feeling is authored by love. Fear writes its own story in me. This is OK. It's part of what it means to be human; an ambivalent creature tossed between love and fear. Only I have to notice the difference between the call of love and the threat of fear. What is moving me to feel the way I do about this decision? Is it love of God or attachment to the world? Some inspirations will not deliver what they promise, no matter how attractive they seem, or how pure. Some will fall apart over time no matter how holy they seem, or how reasonable. One or two of my most sublime experiences will lose their fragrance, no matter how deeply moving and gifted they feel at the time. Only what originates with God will keep its goodness for ever.

## PAUSE AND REFLECT

Discernment of the spirits or various movements we experience in our spiritual life is probably the most neglected area of the Christian faith. It needs to be part of our daily routine, like brushing our teeth. Take ten minutes to notice where in the day and in your prayer you felt drawn to hope and where you felt driven by discouragement. However slight these movements were, it is worth discovering what prompted them. Often this awareness is enough to dispel any discouragement. It also lets you choose to live according to the hope that is within you instead of the fear.

Recognizing that discernment takes time and requires information and self-awareness, the Church of Scotland recently reformed its procedures for selecting candidates for the ordained ministry. Formerly any person who had been a member of the

Church for at least five years could apply to be considered for the ministry at a Selection Conference. The residential conference took place over 48 hours and the applicant underwent interviews, tests and group exercises with fellow applicants. The same conference is still part of the process, but before any applicant gets to test his or her call here they spend around six months exploring it with the help of a co-ordinator. This is a time for information gathering. The applicant is encouraged to find out about the task of ministry, the role of the Church in today's world, the skills they bring to both, and those that need to be developed. The co-ordinator is usually an experienced minister who helps the applicant sift through their experience to discern if the call they are sensing might indeed be a call to ministry.

Most applicants find the period of exploration very useful. Some discover that ministry is not what they thought it was, or that it is not where God is calling them. Others become better informed about the task, but this only serves to make them more determined to offer their service in this way to the Church. Occasionally, however, an applicant appears who sees the exploration period as a hoop to jump through on the way to the Selection Conference. This man or woman has already decided what God's will for them is, and they are not interested in discerning further or even in testing their discernment. They have not the courage of their own conviction. Discernment is not possible without a generous availability to the service of the kingdom. We all need this 'Here I am, is it I?' approach that is both generous and courageous.

## Give us today our daily bread

Here is another petition that requires some courage to pray. With it, Jesus identified the basics for a life lived to the full and in peace. The first thing to notice about this petition for daily bread is the fact that it was not a personal petition. It's not an invitation to God to 'give *me* my daily bread', but a request that God give *us all* daily bread. As we pray this aloud in our churches in the Western world we are not asking for our dietary requirements alone, but also for those in Ethiopia. Shame on us if we have come to expect as a right more than our daily requirements for nurture. Shame on us if we mean give us all the luxury foods we have become accustomed to even if it means others must starve to death today. This is a prayer for the world. Imagine what might happen if we prayed it and actually meant it. God might help us decide what needs to happen so that we can answer it for the world!

Actually the whole prayer is by, and on behalf of, the community. It begins 'Our Father' and this reminds us that discernment is not a way to discover what is best for our interests, but what is in the interests of God's commonwealth.

Most of us discern poorly because we discern selfishly and because we don't want daily bread but the assurance of bread today and bread tomorrow and for all our tomorrows. Living with just enough bread for the day and none for tomorrow is incredibly challenging to those of us with enough wealth and autonomy to plan our futures. Jesus makes no friends among the rich and powerful with this petition.

This reluctance we have to live in the present moment tempts us to make decisions that are not immediately before us. We can certainly do this, but we cannot expect God to help us with them. Once when I was on holiday I attended worship at a city-centre church full of young families and people in their twenties and thirties. The preacher quoted from St Paul, warning single Christians against the dangers of marrying someone who does not share their Christian faith. Paul, of course, was speaking in a particular context believing that Christ's return was imminent. Indeed in a country where Christians are persecuted for their faith one might think twice about marrying someone who did not share one's conviction and could not be expected to shoulder the burden of it. That aside, there is a kind of faith that would make such a marriage difficult. For those who believe that God pre-ordains some of us for salvation and not others, the kindest course of action is to look for a partner among the elect. Once faith becomes more about love (not romantic love but love as freedom) and less concerned with purity laws that include some and exclude others, then marriage between a Christian and an agnostic, a humanist or person of another faith is no longer anathema. Like any marriage it will need hard work to maintain.

But what of the person in the congregation listening to the preacher who resolves not to marry a non-Christian and then meets and is attracted to just such a person? Do they change their earlier decision or stick with it and say goodbye to this potential soul-mate? The difficulty arises because they made a decision that was not actually before them. It has erected a boundary that now the person has to contemplate crossing. Without this earlier resolution there would still be a decision to make but this would be real and involve an actual other person and a here-and-now experience of relationship. Information can be gathered that will help towards a tentative decision, including the advice of the preacher and the guidance of Scripture. Then the Holy Spirit, who is not in the future and is not interested in foretelling it either, will be free to illuminate the path of peace according to his/her hopes for both people, granting each the courage to walk that way.

## Forgive us our debts as we have forgiven those who are in debt to us

In this petition Jesus again draws our attention to the community as the appropriate arena for discernment. When we petition God to forgive our sins we are asking God to forgive not only our personal sins but also the sins of big business, the sins of terrorists and dictators, and celebrities and politicians. We are also inviting God to heal our world of sin in partnership with us. Since God takes our prayer seriously we can expect that in any decision we are discerning that God will honour our desire for a healed world. Scientists who have studied our planet and its chances of survival are telling us that because of our environmental abuse and our aggression the world will turn, is in fact already turning, hostile towards our species. They predict that the world will survive but we will not. 'As we have forgiven' acknowledges that we must become part of the solution to this world's problems in a pro-active spiritual way. Not to do this is like having one foot on the accelerator of a car (forgive us our debts), while having the other foot on the brake (but don't expect us to do our bit).

It doesn't matter how forgiving God is of all our stuff if we are not forgiving both of others and of ourselves. I think this is because sin is really disease. There is no use in God healing the wounds of this world if we insist on picking them open again so that they become infected. We too need to forgive ourselves our poor choices of the past, both individually and corporately. Not to do so seriously inhibits our discernment of present choices because unforgiven people continue to live in fear. The subject of forgiveness could be a book on its own, but we will return to it in Chapter 8 when we look at forgiveness as truth and reconciliation in our personal relationships.

## And do not put us to the test, but save us from the evil one

Fear and temptation are realities of life. Jesus recognizes this, but by addressing them at the end of his lesson on prayer he gives them the necessary attention without exaggerating their significance. During a period of discernment we also need to recognize the presence of fear and temptation so that we can relegate them to the sidelines where they belong. Each of us has a root temptation that tests us. Imagine a tree, then picture the root system beneath it. I know nothing about trees, but I imagine there is among the plethora of roots one main artery. The tree is like all the things we think and say and do that are not recognized by God because God is not in them. But they all stem from that one root temptation and are manifestations of it. This root may develop as a defence strategy; a way of hiding from the answer we have come up with to that misleading question, 'Why am I

61

cast out from paradise?' One person decides they were too pushy in the womb, so they go through life refusing to assert themselves. Another experiences the expulsion as a failure, so they go through life competing with everyone. According to the Enneagram, an ancient system for understanding the self, we all answer this question slightly differently depending not only on our experience in the womb and during birth but also on the nurture received in those crucial early years. Research shows that a child in the womb receives messages from her mother, and through his attitude to wife and unborn child, from her father too. An attitude of ambivalence or deep anxiety about parenthood communicates itself to the unborn child, who from the sixth month on lives as full an emotional life as we do and is beginning to form attitudes and even expectations of herself according to those feelings and perceptions, hopes and fears.

When we make a decision it is tremendously useful to be aware of the particular effect that fear has on us. Perhaps you are tempted by success because you are afraid of failure. Perhaps you are tempted to make choices that keep you in the background because you are a woman used to patriarchs telling you that is where you can serve best. Knowing what tests our faith gives us the opportunity to resist and this can be a simple matter: 'To one of the brethren appeared a devil, transformed into an angel of light, who said to him: I am the Angel Gabriel, and I have been sent to thee. But the brother said: Think again – you must have been sent to somebody else. I haven't done anything to deserve an angel. Immediately the devil ceased to appear' (Merton, 1973).

The evil one we need deliverance from whenever we are trying to make a good decision is this trick our fears have of impersonating God in order to keep us from God. They appear to us like an angel of light; as something holy or wholly reasonable, which persuades us to conform in a multitude of ways to a life that does not have God at its centre. We fall into the hands of this evil when we agree (even with our vote or our thoughts) to ignore forgiveness, inclusiveness and service as though Christ had not been raised and the kingdom was not a reality in this world.

## PAUSE AND REFLECT

What might your root temptation be? Do you know what particular form fear (the root of all sin) takes in your life and how it manages to look like an angel of light? Ask God to show you what your temptation is. It may take some persistence not because God is hiding the truth from you, but because you will want to hide from it – just like Peter refusing to believe that his fear could drive him to deny Jesus. Continue to pray and God will help you to uncover your temptation. The grace to accept the truth about our fear is part of the liberation God has in mind for us.

The prayer that Jesus taught his disciples is a prayer of discernment. It invites us to turn up and abandon our preconceived notions about life, God, self, even about prayer. It challenges us to ask the question 'What if?' and trust God to reveal the answers we need to hear. Some of these will change my mind about God, about the world, about my life, in ways that thinking alone never could. It is useful to note down new insights, along with the ways in which discerning prayer is affecting the decisions you make and put into action. For prayer is more than navel gazing. It leads us to act for the common weal. When we pray we give God the space and the opportunity to show us something new. In return, he/she gives us the grace not to reject that new possibility out of hand because it is different from our image of things or because we are afraid of the truth.

### References

Fleming, David, L., *The Spiritual Exercises of Saint Ignatius – A Literal Translation & A Contemporary Reading.* St Louis, Institute of Jesuit Sources, 3700 West Pine Boulevard, 1980.
Merton, Thomas, *The Wisdom of the Desert.* London, Sheldon Press, 1973.

# 5

## Taking Responsibility

*He did not say 'You will not have a rough time; you will not be burdened; you will not have to face difficulties,' he said, 'You will not be overcome.'*

(Mother Julian of Norwich, 1987 edn)

The man could hardly believe his eyes when he saw the shop sign: 'The Truth Shop'. The salesgirl was attentive: What type of truth did he wish to purchase, partial truth or whole truth? The whole truth was what he wanted; no deceptions, no defences, no rationalizations for him. He would have his truth plain and clear and whole. The salesgirl looked at him compassionately: 'The price is very high, sir,' she told him. 'What is it?' he asked, confident in his desire for the whole truth, whatever the cost. 'The whole truth will cost you your repose for the rest of your life,' she said. The man was like any other. He craved occasional peace and rest in the shelter of his unquestioned beliefs. Was he ready to lose the comfort of familiar defences and rationalizations? He left the store shaking his head sadly.

The truth is that we are the ones responsible for most of the pain we, and those around us, are suffering. Life is often difficult, but every decision we take out of fear makes it more so, even causing us to doubt in God's care for us. The word 'doubt' used in the story of Jesus walking on water, and of Peter's attempt at this, comes from the Greek word that means to look in two different directions. Peter looked at Jesus, but then he caught sight of the waves. He doubted and began immediately to sink below the water. 'Why did you doubt?' (Matthew 14.31) Jesus asks, and it is a good question. Why do we look in two different directions? Love – like walking on water – can seem impossible, and the decision or indecision that fear is suggesting to us can look very reasonable at the time we make it. Being honest enough to recognize this fear at work in us takes a rigorous self-knowledge and a regular discipline of self-examination in the light of the gospel that not too many of us want to acquire.

'A certain brother asked Abbot Pambo: Why do the devils prevent me from doing good to my neighbour? And the elder said to him: Don't talk like that. Is God a liar? Why don't you just admit that you don't want to be merciful? Didn't God say long ago: I have given you power to tread upon serpents and scorpions and on all the forces of the enemy? So why do you not stamp down the evil spirit?' (Merton, 1973).

Ouch. It's tempting to blame God when our decisions turn out badly, especially if they begin well – like Peter's first few steps on the water – but after a time turn sour. 'Why did God let me choose to marry that man?' we ask. Or: 'All the signs led me to believe that this career was God's will for my life' we complain, 'Why give me success to take it away again and leave me in a worse state after so many years of work?' At these times our pride works overtime to justify our choice and deny that we could possibly have made an error of judgement. Pride is a manifestation of fear and it encourages us to hide our nakedness behind some convenient bush.

When David decided to take a census he thought it was a really good idea; inspired by God no less. After all, God had given him many victories over his enemies, had allowed him to amass wealth and power which in turn led to more victories and an even larger kingdom. Why not count the people? He was free to do so and this freedom is indeed inspired by God who gives us all responsibility for our own lives. He was free to count, but God hoped that he wouldn't. He was free to let fear of failure drive his actions, but God hoped that love would draw him as it had in the days of his youth.

Sadly, the man who once wrote 'Happy the people whose God is the LORD' (Psalm 144.15) now found happiness in his increasing power over both his subjects and his enemies. Counting the number of fighting men under his command was a way of underlining this power. It would confirm that he was a successful king who, by his own strength, could keep what he had gained.

As soon as the last man was counted, David knew in his heart he had made a mistake. He had misused the freedom God had given him; had served his own fears rather than the cause of love. What makes David so interesting is his willingness to face the facts: 'I have sinned greatly in what I have done. But now, O LORD, I pray thee, take away the iniquity of thy servant; for I have done very foolishly' (2 Samuel 24.10).

## PAUSE AND REFLECT

Think of a decision you made which at the time seemed in some way inspired by God, but later turned out badly. Try to face the facts of the matter, and pray to God for the grace to be as honest as you can about your motives. The more significant the decision, the more difficult it is to be honest – so start with something not too important.

When my family and I moved to rural Aberdeenshire from the central belt of Scotland the children were aged eleven, seven and three. The eleven-year-old settled quickly, as did the three-year-old, but the seven-year-old missed the town and missed the doorbell ringing with chums inviting him out to play. How could I help him to settle? Time would have done the trick. New friends would have appeared and new freedoms been discovered. But I could not wait, and decided to buy a dog. We had never had one before, but now seemed the perfect time and place; indeed, a neighbour was offering me a puppy and the idea caused a great deal of excitement among all three children. Homesickness was forgotten as we bought the dog-basket, bowl, blanket and dog-lead. Excitement reached fever pitch when we drove to the farm to collect the chosen one. There was just one problem. I do not like dogs! Within a month we had discovered that my dislike was shared by the whole family. None of us likes dogs, and certainly not our own. My son was still homesick.

Even with such a trivial example it can be hard to be honest. Didn't God send the neighbour to me in the first place to plant the seed of this plan? Wasn't the house and situation ideal for a dog? Surely my willingness to 'have a go' should have guaranteed the success of my rescue attempt? How could buying a dog possibly be a sin?

The truth is that my own happiness at the move to Aberdeen-shire contrasted starkly with my son's unhappiness and I felt guilty as well as helpless. I needed to rescue him and me and to do it quickly. But my decision was not really the creative act I wanted to believe it was. It wasn't even a good decision for the dog.

Be careful now. The point in looking back is not to beat ourselves up about decisions already made. Remember that repentance is not feeling bad about our past, but thinking differently in the present. This can help us sort out an unwise decision or live with it gracefully, just as David acquiesced to the very difficult consequences of his census. It was Gad, the king's seer, who brought the bad news:

So Gad came to David and told him, and said to him, 'Shall three years of famine come to you in your land? Or will you flee three months before your foes while they pursue you? Or shall there be three days' pestilence in your land? Now consider, and decide what answer I shall return to him who sent me.' Then David said to Gad, 'I am in great distress; let us fall into the hand of the Lord, for his mercy is great; but let me not fall into the hand of man.' (2 Samuel 24.13–14)

David's own foolishness and pride has brought him to the kind of hard choice we were exploring earlier. I am not for a moment suggesting that God punishes us like this, but the people of David's time thought he did and hence this story. What I want us to notice is how differently David is already thinking about himself in relation to God. In choosing to put himself in the hands of the Lord he once more discovers and demonstrates the trust in God that made him a great king.

Once we recognize the fear that motivated our choice it is time to move on and to do this we need to forgive ourselves. The grace to live as forgiven people is one that God is always generous in giving. If we have not taken advantage of the gift, perhaps it is because we are mistakenly worshipping a God who loves only perfect people, not those in the process of becoming perfectly human. The woman whose tears mingled with the expensive ointment she used to soothe her Lord's feet had been taught to think of God in this way. Then she met Jesus. The bitter regret she felt for her many poor decisions gave way to profound joy when she encountered in him the breadth and depth and sheer optimism of God's letting-be; God's compassionate love for her. Jesus tells the disbelieving Pharisees: 'For this reason I tell you that her sins, her many sins, must have been forgiven her, or she would not have shown such great love. It is the man who is forgiven little who shows little love' (Luke 7.47, Jerusalem Bible). Those who are forgiven much are deeply joyful in their response, whether they are singing in church services or pouring expensive oil over Jesus' feet. Joy like this helps us to stop hiding from the plain truth that we are our own worst enemies.

## PAUSE AND REFLECT

The grace to face the truth about ourselves and then live as a forgiven person is one we all need to ask for on a daily basis. It follows on from the discernment of spirits where we took a few minutes at night to look over the day and notice the movement of love within us and the movement of fear. Now we ask the Holy Spirit to help us notice the thoughts, words and deeds that sprang from faith and those that were our flight or fight response to fear. This examination of the day will prompt you to give thanks for the former and say 'sorry' for the latter. Consider what grace you need to help you love more tomorrow and then ask for this. When you waken, thank God for the new day given to you because in it you are free to praise, reverence and serve God. This is what it means to be forgiven. Ask again for the grace you have identified to help you do this, e.g. more patience or self-control or generosity. All of this will take as long as your journey from bed to bathroom. When you get there, greet the forgiven person you see in the mirror.

If we can be honest about small matters, like being irritable with colleagues or selfish with our time, this will help us to be more honest about those big decisions that are causing us pain. Marriage is perhaps the most difficult decision to be this honest about. We want to believe that a high divorce rate is the result of a relaxation of divorce laws. This is less distressing than contemplating the possibility that divorce generally dissolves a marriage that was not the best choice for either person in the first place. If we have a lovely home, a beautiful family, a wide circle of friends, it is hard to discover that we married this man or this woman under some kind of psychological duress. Our problem is not that divorce is too easy, but that marriage is. It is the easiest thing in the world to marry for the wrong reasons. Perhaps she was afraid to be left on the shelf in an era when the worth of a woman was pretty much defined by her marriage status. Perhaps he was escaping from an overbearing mother while unconsciously seeking out an overbearing wife as replacement. What should a person do when they discover that this major decision was not in fact God's choice for them?

There is no formulaic answer, but a good first step is to do what David did. David could have continued to justify his census to himself, claiming that God told him to take it, or pointing to all the good that had come from it. But David has lived long in a relationship of trust with God and he is not afraid to confess his mistake and ask for forgiveness. David's confession chimes with the advice of Ignatius:

> If it becomes apparent that the choice or decision has not been made as it should have been and if there has been a certain disordered attachment involved, our first response is one of sorrow and an attempt to amend by putting our efforts into righting the situation. Professional help or the help of friends who can be objective, along with a legitimate authority itself, must oftentimes play an important role at this time of re-evaluation.
>
> There is no sense trying to say God's call is directly involved in a choice which we have made because of a disordered attachment. For the call from God is not at the whim of faulty information, sensual emotion, or disordered love.
>
> (Fleming, 1980)

This strikes me as incredibly modern advice from a man who lived 500 years ago. How liberating it is to face with courage the disordered decisions we have made in the past and justified over and over again. What a relief to step off that particular merry-go-round of self-deceit and accept God's forgiveness by forgiving ourselves.

Putting one's efforts into 'righting the situation' will mean making some decisions about the future. Perhaps a woman feels inclined to end her marriage. This may be a good decision, but it is not one to be taken lightly. It would be wise to discern this next step carefully. Here is some guidance from the prayer Jesus taught us:

*Our Father in heaven:* Discernment begins when we become aware that the God we are praying to for help with our decision is the God who will do what love requires. (Note: Sometimes a woman feels she must stay in an abusive marriage because of the sacred nature of marriage vows taken. What does this say about her Father in heaven?)

*May your name be held holy:* Remember that to keep God's name holy we must seek to find 'what God calls me to at this time of my life' (Fleming, 1980). Perhaps you want to walk free from a relationship that is less than creative. If you make this your goal, you fall into the error of putting means before ends. It's a mistake we all make: declaring to God that we will keep his/her name holy once our own goals are satisfied. God may want what we want, but the purpose of discernment is to discover God's preference and this won't happen if we pre-judge the matter. And God honours our previous decisions by working with even the poorest of them in a creative way. It may be that God is calling you to reform your vows with a new, more realistic, vision of marriage and a more clear-sighted view of your partner. How will you know if you have already settled on your own will?

*Your kingdom come, your will be done:* To discover God's will for us and for the community both local and universal it is useful to do some information gathering. In the question of a marriage this may include attending marriage counselling sessions together. A couple may discover that they have married the right person for the wrong reasons, or that in the passing of years they are becoming the right partners for one another. They may decide that it is worth persevering together in mutual respect, if not passion, for the sake of the children, at least until the youngest turns 25 and finally flies the nest. Or it may become clear that God hopes they can make a good, compassionate end to their relationship. I cannot tell you what will happen if you seek God's will for you in this situation. I can only assure you that the one who seeks always finds out what God's hope for them is.

*Give us today our daily bread:* We discern poorly when we discern selfishly. Decisions made about marriage affect a community of people and special care needs to be taken so that what we want does not deprive someone, either directly or indirectly, of the basics of nurture and security and dignity.

*And forgive us our debts, as we have forgiven those who are in debt to us:* Whether the marriage endures or not, the grace to forgive ourselves and our partner is essential if our wounds are ever to heal. Remember that unforgiven and unforgiving people continue to live in fear and make decisions from fear. To discern the way ahead you need to let Christ begin the process of healing.

*And do not put us to the test, but save us from the evil one:* Stay alert to the realities of fear and temptation in your life and the habit these have of impersonating God. It may look very holy or wholly reasonable to sacrifice your own chance for happiness in life for the sake of the marriage vows you made, but a decision is only holy if it is of God. So test your aspirations to see if they bring you real peace or a mocking counterfeit.

We can minimize the chance of future regrets if we learn to notice when we are at peace with a tentative decision and when we are feigning this. Contemplating the life of Jesus is the only way I know to learn what peace actually is. The peace he gives us is distinct: 'Peace I leave with you; my peace I give to you; not as the world gives do I give to you. Let not your hearts be troubled, neither let them be afraid' (John 14.27), but it is not exclusive to those called to retreat from the world. People with busy lives that are lived in public places and noisy homes are included in the circle of his concern. We too can know his peace.

If we use our imagination and the 'What if?' question in prayer to flesh out the Gospel accounts of Jesus' life, then we will notice the difference between the peace of mind that the world offers us (at a price) and the peace of Christ.

72

## PAUSE AND REFLECT

Read the passage in John 20.19–23 where Jesus appears to his companions as they hide in the upper room a few days after his awful death. Take time to set the scene as though you are a film director: picturing the dimensions and shape of the room, any furniture, the floor covering, the walls and position of any windows, the door. Imagine the atmosphere, and even smell the smells of grief and fear, among the men and women. Perhaps there is loud wailing or quiet sobs. Try to imagine yourself present and notice where you are in the room and what you are doing. Then, when you have some sense of this confused gathering of people lost in private regrets, let Christ appear. Notice the reaction and imagine what yours might be. Do you move forward to meet him or hang back? Listen to the words Jesus speaks and hear them as though he is addressing them to you. If you want to ask him anything do so, and listen to his response. Repeat this contemplation each time you come to prayer until you begin to understand what it is about peace that Christ is concerned to share with his friends and with you.

People who spend time getting to know Jesus by interacting with Scripture in this contemplative way discover that for them, as for him, peace is a river of gratitude that flows from decisions we make that are inclusive, empowering to those who have been told they are worthless, and merciful to those whose own fears drive them to violence or lies. Wherever this river flows, it produces an increase of faith in the God who lets-be, of hope for God's vision of a commonwealth of free human beings, and of love that sets us free from our fears to serve this kingdom of peace.

By contrast, peace of mind consists of insurance against various probable futures. We may get sick, we may lose our employment, if we live long enough we will get old, and inevitably the day will come when we die. Health insurance, pension funds, savings; all of these can buy us peace of mind, at least until the markets fall.

What if the rich young ruler had assured Jesus not that he had kept all the Commandments, but that he had made every provision for the future? Imagine that he had investment plans for his children's education, pensions arranged for himself and his partner, retirement homes lined up for his parents, funeral plans for them all, as well as a plethora of policies insuring him against every conceivable calamity. What if Jesus suggested not only that he follow him – which, after all, the disciples had done before him – but that he cash in his policies and give the proceeds to the poor? Try to imagine how incredulous the man might have felt at this absurd piece of advice. No wonder he shook his head sadly as he turned away. He had just realized how dangerously insane Jesus really was.

Or contemplate Lazarus' sister Martha who worked hard for her peace of mind. She was 'anxious and troubled about many things' (Luke 10.41) and this left her exhausted, irritated and confused. Surely she deserves a bit of peace for all her trouble. Jesus tells her that few things need concern her; indeed, only one. He does not say what this one thing is; Martha has to discover it, and choose it for herself. So do we.

There is no great mystery to the peace Christ wants us to share, but you can be sure that there is a certain absurdity to it. That is why, like David taking his census, we tend to doubt that it is sensible to place all our faith in such an absurd God. So we hedge our bets with some faith in other gods too. We count on science, technology, hard work or even our own luck to secure the happiness/security/love we feel we deserve.

This all looks so sensible that we do not notice that our faith, hope and love are shrivelling up; becoming dry and hard. Martha did not notice this when she complained about her sister to Jesus: 'Lord, do you not care that my sister has left me to serve alone? Tell her then to help me' (Luke 10.40). She had made the wrong choice for herself and now she wants to blame her sister for the turmoil and uncertainty and resentment that is growing in her. I wonder how Martha reacted when Jesus told her to stop worrying about things that don't matter. She probably went muttering into the kitchen that 'It's not as simple as all that in spite of what Jesus thinks!'

Life is seldom simple. When it is at its most difficult and our choice lies between one heartache and another it can be hard to hold on to the faith Martha was later to profess: that God can bring life out of death. I do not know what hard decisions you have had to make already, but I do know people who have chosen between living with an alcoholic partner or breaking up the family, coping with a confused elderly parent alone or putting her in a nursing home, undergoing painful treatment for cancer or refusing treatment and letting the illness take its course. That people in these circumstances do hold on by the tips of their fingers, as Martha and Mary did when their brother Lazarus died, is an encouragement to the rest of us.

At times like these it is all the more important to know that God is neither testing us to see if we are his good little children, nor biting divine nails like an anxious mother afraid to watch us make matters worse for ourselves. Nor has God abandoned us, though the stress we are under can make God feel distant and our attempts at prayer futile. God trusts us to decide and knows that we can only do this on the basis of the revelation of love we have personally received from Christ.

Nevertheless, it is given to some to be the keepers of the revelation, the storytellers of God's love for us all. Mother Julian of Norwich, a fourteenth-century anchoress, was one of these saints. The first woman to write a book in the English language, her *Revelations of Divine Love* offers straightforward and compassionate guidance as we seek to understand God's way with a world that all too often can seem full of nothing but suffering.

Keeping company with saints like Mother Julian, by reading their work and making their prayers our own, can give us the courage to make even the most difficult decisions. The 16 'shew-ings' that formed the basis of her theology of love were given in an intense spiritual experience. When it was over, Julian sensed Jesus reassuring her that they were no delusion but a revelation she could trust: 'Accept it, believe it, hold on to it, be encouraged by it and trust it: and you will not be overcome' (Mother Julian of Norwich, 1987 edn). Mother Julian wrote to encourage people like us to be as assured by these words as she was and to trust our own experience of God's love even at those times when we do not sense God's presence. Trusting that we will not be overcome gives us courage, no matter how difficult the situation or how ambiva-lent we feel about our choice:

> Do not be afraid, for I have redeemed you;
> I have called you by your name, you are mine.
> Should you pass through the sea, I will be with you;
> Or through rivers, they will not swallow you up.
> Should you walk through fire, you will not be scorched
> And the flames will not burn you.
> For I am Yahweh, your God,
> The Holy One of Israel, your saviour.
>                     (Isaiah 43.2–3, Jerusalem Bible)

In these poetic verses the captive people of Israel are not imme-diately removed from the 'rough times' they experience in the grasp of ruthless military powers. Instead, God promises they will not be overcome by the dangers they face. When we face agonizing decisions these verses remind us that God knows the utmost extent of our dilemma and the necessity of making a choice. They promise that if we have the courage to make a deci-sion, we will also find within ourselves the grace to live with it.

This grace can be experienced as an unexpected peace or a sense of rightness in our decision. We may be aware of our own courage or fortitude and know that this is what it means to have God claim us as his/her own. God is determined to accompany us through every extreme and this alone is enough to transform the most difficult trial into a meaningful part of our quest. At times we cannot discern the way ahead with any degree of peace, but nevertheless respond to God's love by making as good a decision as we are able. Then God tells us not to be afraid of making a mistake since he/she has redeemed all of our mistakes.

We can and do choose wrongly for the best of reasons, but this is often when we discover that God is able to do more than we can ever imagine possible with our ambivalent love. Meanwhile, one decision – however hard it is to make – leads on to another, and in adversity life favours those brave enough to keep faith with God's peaceful commonwealth no matter how dimly they perceive it. Courage in the face of adversity is a choice that says more about us than our abilities do or the circumstances in which we find ourselves. And God says, 'Do not be afraid.'

## References

Fleming, David L., *The Spiritual Exercises of Saint Ignatius – A Literal Translation & A Contemporary Reading*. St Louis, Institute of Jesuit Sources, 3700 West Pine Boulevard, 1980.

Merton, Thomas, *The Wisdom of the Desert*. London, Sheldon Press, 1973.

Mother Julian of Norwich, *Revelations of Divine Love*. London, Hodder & Stoughton Christian Classics, 1987.

# 6

# *Going Global*

———⸺◦◦◦⸺———

*Real choice both expresses and curtails freedom – or rather it should lead us further and further away from a picture of choice that presupposes a blank will looking out at a bundle of options like goods on a supermarket shelf.*

(Williams, 2003)

A wealthy businessman on his way to an important meeting stood in an airport, feeling quite concerned about missing his plane. His watch wasn't working and he couldn't find a clock, so he asked another man to tell him the time. The stranger obliged, setting down two large heavy-looking cases to look at his own watch. 'It's precisely 5:09, the outside temperature is 68 degrees, and it will rain later. In New York the sky is clear and the temperature there is 75 degrees. Here in London the moon will be full tonight and the barometer reading is . . .' The businessman interrupted, incredulous, 'Your watch tells you all that?' 'It does, and much more,' replied the man. 'I'll give you 1,000 dollars for it right now,' said the businessman and was disappointed when the stranger declined the offer. 'I couldn't possibly sell this watch. I invented it, you see; it's the only one in the world and I intend to give it to my son for his twenty-first birthday.' But the wealthy traveller was determined to have the watch and so he offered 2,000 dollars for it. The inventor stayed resolute: 'It's not for sale,' and he reached down to pick up his suitcases. 'Now wait,' said the other man, 'I'll pay you 10,000 dollars and I have the cash right here,' and he reached for his wallet. At the stranger paused and once more set down his suitcases: 'Ten thousand dollars? OK, it's a deal.' The traveller was delighted, paid for the watch, took it and snapped it on his wrist, thanked the inventor, and turned to leave. 'Wait a minute,' the stranger said and handed the two cases to the man. 'Don't forget the batteries.'

That we are free to make decisions about the direction of our life is not simply a matter of psychological and spiritual development. Freedom is a matter of economics. The more wealth we have, the more decisions we can make. But have you noticed that the greater the choice our wealth grants us, the more foolish the choices we prove ourselves capable of making? Perhaps few of us would be tempted by the wristwatch in the story but we are enthralled by mobile phones that take photos, send texts and emails and even let us play games. Because the technology is available and affordable gimmicks become indispensable – must-have accessories to modern life. Or take television channels. Never before have there been so many channels to choose from but they are mostly filled with programmes of mind-numbingly poor quality. This, however, doesn't stop us from beaming them into our homes where we select one dire option after another.

A society of blank wills looking to a pre-packaged selection of options for retail therapy is not what God has in mind for us. God is creating a commonwealth, but we are settling for a commercial cult that mesmerizes with bells and whistles so effectively that we fail to notice the heavy baggage that comes with it. Erich Fromm describes this burden: 'We are proud that we are not subject to any external authority, that we are free to express our thoughts and feelings, and we take it for granted that this freedom almost automatically guarantees our individuality' (Fromm, 1942). He then goes on to sound a warning note that is even more relevant now than when Fromm sounded it 40 years ago: 'The right to express our thoughts, however, means something only if we are able to have thoughts of our own.'

Forty years ago the town I grew up in had no supermarkets. Shopping was done in the town high street, going in and out of one shop after another. It took a couple of hours to queue to be served in the butcher's shop, the fishmonger, the baker, the grocery, the chemist, the delicatessen and the fruit and vegetable stall in the market. Each new purchase added to the load carried from shop to shop. It was a time-consuming and, in a British winter, miserable chore – though it could also be a sociable one and, compared to shopping trends today, it did benefit the environment. Folk bought only what they could carry, often travelling to and from the shopping centre on public transport, and were prepared to carry only what was needed to provide a healthy balanced diet for the family. This meant there was little waste at home and only limited demand for luxury items in the shops.

Supermarkets transformed the shopping experience offering the convenience and comfort of visiting one shop, loading a trolley with everything needed, usually pre-packaged, and queuing only once to pay. Their buying power meant a vast range and choice of products, both necessities and luxuries, at affordable prices. Advertising in the shops and through the growing media industry cultivated a new type of customer. Though the needs of this customer for a balanced diet and clothes and shoes appropriate for each season remained unchanged, the appetite for more had growth potential. With some might say sinister patience the advertising industry has cultivated our trust and gradually developed society's appetite for more. It has taken less than 40 years to convince us that choice is our right; that it is reasonable to expect the best of everything and that to live is to have. Supermarkets are the new cathedrals.

## PAUSE AND REFLECT

We know that teenagers spend years freeing themselves from the external authority of parents while submitting to the less obvious control exerted by their peers. What if you unwittingly conform in thoughts, words and actions to authorities not as visible as those like the Church and the state, but even more powerful? Consider (or ask some teenagers you know) how advertisers make use of peer pressure (fear of exclusion) to sell products and cultivate consumers. How might the unfettered power of the free market rob you of the ability to make free choices while concealing this fact from you?

In this consumerist society waste is a huge problem for the developed world, while cash crops lay waste poorer countries, stripping them of even the little wealth they have. And it has all happened so quickly. The kind of free enterprise that accords our 'right to choose' the highest moral value in any situation is rushing us headlong towards disaster, but turning back is as hard for us as for the lemmings. Attempts were made 11 years ago at the first Earth Summit in Rio, but most of the measures agreed there to help sustain the planet were never implemented.

In 1992 the world had 600 million motor vehicles, most of them in cities in the developed world; today we have more than 1 billion motor vehicles. We have, after all, the right to choose private transport rather than public for ourselves and our families.

The rainforest, which in 1992 was being depleted at a rate of 179,000 square kilometres a year, is currently disappearing at 1 per cent per year. We have, after all, the right to encourage countries like Costa Rica to service our consumer choices by tearing down its forests to make more room for rearing cows, which are then exported to the United States and made into hamburgers. The average American cat consumes more beef in a year than most Costa Rican citizens do.

The world has 3 million more refugees and spends £20 billion more than the £606 billion of global military spending in 1992. We choose to ignore the tension between those who have choice and those from whom we take choice, defending this right with weapons of mass destruction and policing it with our immigration laws.

Ten years on, at the Earth Summit held in Johannesburg in 2002, sustainable development was the main topic of discussion. How can we continue to increase consumption, and therefore economic growth, without turning the Earth into a rubbish tip? Or how can we have our cake and eat it too? Perhaps there is another question we could more usefully address if only we could find the courage to ask it. What if capitalism, the decision to have rather than to serve, has passed its shelf life? In his opening speech to the summit, Thabo Mbeki told the delegates: 'A global human society based on poverty for many and prosperity for a few, characterized by islands of wealth surrounded by a sea of poverty, is unsustainable.'

Of course it is. We know this is true and we know what it means in each situation of choice. The problem is not that we do not know what the sustainable action is, but that we are afraid to take it. A leper once approached Jesus. While the crowd scattered or averted their eyes and some began to shout abuse at the unfortunate man, Jesus walked forward to meet him: 'If you will, you can make me clean' (Mark 1.40), the leper said. 'Moved with pity, he stretched out his hand and touched him, and said to him, "I will; be clean"' (Mark 1.41). We too have the means to heal much of the world's wounds and those of its people. All we lack is the will.

## PAUSE AND REFLECT

Earth can be a place of ease for a few and hardship for most, or it can be a place of modest comfort for us all. Read the story of the poor man and Lazarus in Luke's Gospel. In the light of this Gospel story, pray to understand how Christ might define 'ease', 'hardship', 'the few', 'the many' and 'comfort'. What do you want the Earth to be? What are you doing, at home, at work, at play and at worship, to help heal the disease of planet Earth and of the poorest inhabitant on it? What might you do to help the Earth become a sustainable home for everyone?

We all know that it would be good to leave our cars at home and take public transport, or at least share our cars with neighbours making the same daily journey to work. We know that every time we start up a car engine, the life of someone else's child becomes a little more difficult; the air she breathes more polluted, the debt she is burdened with a bit deeper. We choose to ignore this because private transport is quicker, cleaner and, well, more private. The commercial cult has programmed us to care more about our personal convenience and our personal space than we do about the long-term effects of irresponsible decisions on our beleaguered planet and her people. So much so that nations will go to war in order to defend their supply of oil at a price they are prepared to pay.

The speed of the Earth's progress towards annihilation calls to mind those fabulous domino tracks that people set up. Once that first domino is tipped over we watch open-mouthed as the wave of falling dominos sweeps across the room, splitting off in multiple directions, climbing obstacles, and only stopping when the last domino has fallen. The decisions we make as individuals and as communities have a domino effect. Things that affect one person directly affect all others indirectly.

Who knew this better than King David?

It happened towards evening when David had risen from his couch and was strolling on the palace roof, that he saw from the roof a woman bathing; the woman was very beautiful. David made inquiries about this woman and was told, 'Why, that is Bathsheba, Eliam's daughter, the wife of Uriah the Hittite'. Then David sent messengers and had her brought. She came to him, and he slept with her; now she had just purified herself from her courses. She then went home again. The woman conceived and sent word to David, 'I am with child'. (2 Samuel 11.2–5, Jerusalem Bible)

It was supposed to be a one-night stand enjoyed by a powerful man whose right to choose was absolute. Now he was forced to make other decisions and involve more people. Having decided to entertain himself with Bathsheba, he now tries to pass off the fruit of the affair as Uriah's own child. When this does not work he gives instructions to Joab to see to it that Uriah is placed in the thick of battle and left with no support, for David has decided to have the soldier killed then take Bathsheba for his wife. The plan works, though Uriah is not the only one to die; other lives are already being affected by the king's decisions. Bathsheba mourns her husband and then David marries her. That seemed to be the end of the matter until Nathan comes to speak to David.

He tells the king a story of a poor man who was robbed of his one ewe lamb by a rich man who, though he had plenty of sheep, refused to kill one of these to feed a visitor. 'Instead he took the poor man's lamb and prepared it for his guest' (2 Samuel 12.4, Jerusalem Bible). David was outraged: '"As Yahweh lives," he said to Nathan "the man who did this deserves to die!"' (2 Samuel 12.5.) Having committed himself to this judgement, David has no leg to stand on when Nathan reveals, '"You are the man"' (2 Samuel 12.7, Jerusalem Bible). He goes on:

Thus Yahweh speaks, 'I will stir up evil for you out of your own House. Before your very eyes I will take your wives and give them to your neighbour, and he shall lie with your wives in the sight of this sun. You worked in secret, I will work this in the face of all Israel and in the face of the sun.'

David said to Nathan, 'I have sinned against Yahweh'. Then Nathan said to David, 'Yahweh, for his part, forgives your sin; you are not to die. Yet because you have outraged Yahweh by doing this, the child that is born to you is to die.' (2 Samuel 12.11–14, Jerusalem Bible)

To give David his due, he does recognize the sin in his life and does not rage against the consequences of it. When Bathsheba's son fell ill, 'David pleaded with Yahweh for the child; he kept a strict fast and went home and spent the night on the bare ground, covered with sacking' (2 Samuel 12.16, Jerusalem Bible). But when on the seventh day the child died, David did not wring his hands and cry 'Why me?' Instead he accepted both his responsibility and God's forgiveness. Later he and Bathsheba conceived another son and they called him Solomon.

We too are the man. Refusing to curtail the freedom our wealth gives us we rob the poor of a sustainable future for our immediate satisfaction. I was as outraged as David recently when I learned that in India water is currently being pumped into a soft drinks plant to wash bottles and to manufacture the drink itself. In villages around the plant women walk several miles twice a day to collect and carry two seven-gallon containers of water from a well to keep their families alive. Meanwhile, I pop the well-known product into my supermarket trolley without a thought. It is not expensive. Cheap food and drink and fuel is our right, and we exercise our right to have these as though we were absolute monarchs.

## PAUSE AND REFLECT

It is easy to take our freedom to choose for granted because it depends so much on the circumstances into which we were born. In *Say To This Mountain* we are confronted with a long list of issues about which we have choice. The list includes:

Where to live, how to earn a living, which school your children attend, what to wear today, whether to eat today or take a shower, whether to save money and how much, whether to buy medicines prescribed for you or your family, where to go on holiday, how to improve your home or make it more beautiful, whether to repair what is broken in your home, what to do with your inheritance, to own a car or not, to have a phone or not, where to go on holiday.

Reflect on the meaning and importance of each one for you and try to imagine how it would feel *not* to have the option to choose.

No doubt you will be able to add to this list.

The islands of wealth that President Mbeki speaks about are sparsely populated, while the seas of poverty are teeming. Very few of Christ's brothers and sisters will ever be in a position to make any of the choices you and I make. Bob Geldof became involved in the issue of Third World debt when he realized that people do not die of drought, but politics. Jesus said the poor would always be with us (due to natural scarcity and personal misfortune), but while he took pity on them, we write them off with protectionist policies both national and international that are neither natural nor humane. In Britain homelessness is a political choice. Though we have eternity in common with the person sleeping in a doorway, we deny him affordable housing in order to keep more of what we have to ourselves.

The faith of Jesus challenges this attitude. 'What does it profit a man to gain the whole world and forfeit his life?' (Mark 8.36) he asks. The world is not ours to have but to serve. We can have rights or we can serve the rights of others. We can have goods or we can serve the common good. We can have aspirations or we can serve God's commonwealth. Jesus was clear that if we save up for ourselves all the trappings that we think make life worth living we will lose our humanity. Only by giving away the rights we think we have to our possessions and aspirations can we know what life really is. Or, as Stanley Hauerwas tells us in his discussion of Christian ethics, 'Discipleship is quite simply extended training in being dispossessed' (Hauerwas, 1983).

When it comes to making decisions that affect our environment – and most of our decisions do affect our environment in some way sooner or later – if we continue to insist on our right to possess we will forfeit the planet. Those who choose to live in God's common-wealth surrender this right. They make decisions from the dispos-sessed position that nothing is ours; not the oil we refine nor the minerals we extract, not the water we drink nor the air we breathe. We are not even managers or stewards of these things, in case we thought we had some colonialist-type power to exert. We are the recipients of many wonderful gifts that we have not earned and can never deserve. The decisions we make will be good, will matter to God if they reflect the profound gratitude we experience when we consider the mercy that God continues to pour out on his/her creation. When we stop hoarding we will be free to serve the needs (as opposed to the appetites) of one another.

Training in dispossession is not an immediately attractive proposition, but then the annihilation of the planet doesn't have much to commend it either. Faced with a choice between these two an individual can feel helpless. Even if we found the courage to live the faith of Jesus, where would we begin?

It is reasonable to expect that those elected to represent us at world summits and on bodies like the World Trade Organization will express our determination for a just world. Often they don't, and this can be because we have not made our priorities clear. Democracy is not just about elected representation. We cannot cast our vote and then go home to become carping spectators. Our lively and determined presence is the main artery of democracy. While politicians negotiated the end of apartheid, shoppers stopped buying produce from South Africa. Supermarkets were forced to supply their stores with an alternative source of tinned fruits, and no doubt these conglomerates began to make their pres-ence felt to the politicians. It took time, of course, but the collapse of apartheid was inevitable as soon as the people decided to end it.

More recently, Larry Elliott of the *Guardian* wrote that:

The Jubilee 2000 campaign for debt relief only succeeded after many years of spadework in which all the claims of the lobbyists were rejected by the tight wads in the G7 who first insisted that there was no problem, then that debt relief would only make matters worse; then that it should be limited in its generosity. Eventually, after civil society was mobilized by the churches across the west, the battle was won.

Jubilee 2000, which in Britain involved the trade unions, the Jewish, Muslim and Hindu communities as well as the secular aid agencies and the Christian Church, illustrates the power for transformation that each of us has when we make our presence and our priorities known. We could do the same in any other area of life in which we chose to make the faith of Jesus present.

Take the tourism industry. Holidays are one of those luxuries that we are encouraged to think of as a basic human right and for a very good reason. Tourism is currently the world's biggest business with around 625 million people travelling internationally every year. Two weeks in the sun is the right of all who work hard the other 50 weeks of the year – but do I really think that, or did you think it for me? Either way, when we go abroad we have come to expect a Western standard of accommodation, food, hygiene and safety whichever continent we choose to patronize with our travellers' cheques. So long as standards are met we are content, and happily close our eyes to any social deprivation lying outside the tourist compounds or to the environmental impact our holidays have on the lives of our hosts. Is this attitude one of having or of serving?

If taking a holiday abroad is a creative action it will be good not just for business in the West, or for jaded workers who need a break. It will be a creative way of serving the people whose countries we visit. It will benefit their economy without costing them their environment. It will nurture friendship between cultures without condoning human rights abuses. If our holiday serves a purpose that matters, it will improve the life of even the most powerless citizen in that country. Travel can do all of these things, but not perhaps when the 'package' holiday invites us to abdicate responsibility for all the details. The brochure tells us everything it is wise for us to know about our resort and nothing that might disturb our enjoyment. Simply book the holiday most convenient and pay for it. No need to think about how much fuel is being used to take you to your destination – just pay the fuel tax, itself kept to a minimum by politicians worried about their jobs.

Can you imagine Jesus booking a holiday for himself like this? We know he did take a holiday with his family and it may have been an annual break. They travelled to Jerusalem for the Passover festival. It was a pilgrimage, but exciting and recreational for all that. When Jesus visited Jerusalem as an adult with a bunch of his friends he saw the holiday with new eyes. The wholesale slaughter of animals, the profiteering of the money changers, struck him as something to be deplored. Holy days were times of special prayer; an opportunity to retreat from daily toil to meet God. This is how a person recreates himself or herself – not through excess and frantic queuing to see the sights and hear the sounds of man making money.

This time when he went on holiday, Jesus wanted to know about the people he met and how they lived and what problems they faced. We can know these things too if we take the trouble to enquire. *The Green Travel Guide* is a useful book to read, while the Sustainable Tourism Initiative, an international programme backed by the United Nations, can answer some of our questions as they help developing countries to protect their environment while extending a welcome to tourists. At the very least, we can find out what percentage of the money spent by tourists in a country like India stays in that country to help the local people and how much finds its way into the coffers of Western tourism companies without benefiting the local people at all. Isn't this what the Christian community is really about?

A few years ago my family and I enjoyed a holiday in France.

One day we took the train into Paris and, as we came up from the Gard du Nord railway station on to the pavement, the first thing that we saw, just 20 yards further along the road, was a McDonald's restaurant. How disappointed we felt seeing that familiar sign. As we looked beyond it we recognized other shop signs and wondered if we really were in Paris or if the train had in fact taken us beneath the Channel and deposited us back in any one of our British cities.

Still the news was not *all* bad. Our stomachs and our children told us it was lunchtime, and the sight of McDonald's, though it disappointed, also reassured us that we could feed our young children without having to venture into the unknown world of French culture and cuisine. An hour later (for thankfully the term 'fast food' does not translate into French no matter what you order) we exited from the restaurant, fuelled and ready to see the same sights that every other tourist that day would be queuing up to view. The word 'franchise' means in the first instance 'the right to vote', and therefore denotes the freedom and privilege enjoyed in a democracy. But in commerce the word 'franchise' is the authorization a manufacturer grants to a distributor to market a product in a way that is uniform to the manufacturer's stipulations. McDonald's is a very successful example of a franchise. Wherever you go in the world, McDonald's offers the same meals in the same environment. It's a disturbing thought.

As disturbing as the disappointment I feel when I visit a town for the first time in Britain only to discover that the shops are the same ones I left back home. There is little diversity to be seen any more in our town centres; scant evidence of the uniqueness of place and endeavour; the skills and imagination of individual human beings who live there and nowhere else. The trend towards uniformity makes me uneasy. It doesn't raise my spirits. It fails to elicit from me a grateful gasp of wonder, could never direct me to the God of diversity behind all creation.

Our global human society is a commercial cult enjoyed by a few and endured by many. In this cult I am free to elect my own goals, but these turn out to be the same as everyone else's. This uniformity of franchise masquerades as the unity of freedom, not only in politics and economics but also in religion.

Over the last five years courses in the basics of Christianity have enjoyed brisk business, first in the United Kingdom and then in an international market. Enthusiasts are greatly encouraged by the number of people professing faith in Christ after attending them. Television programmes have explored the attraction of what they call the spin-doctors' version of the gospel. In one, a smartly dressed, upwardly mobile gentlemen, looking like a modern version of the rich young ruler, smiles into the camera. He explains that before doing the course, he thought that embracing Christianity would entail a ludicrous leap of faith, resulting in him having to adopt a lifestyle of mohair jumpers and open-toed sandals. What a relief to discover that neither the ludicrous leap nor the ludicrous clothes were necessary.

I wonder. The Christian community has a great deal to offer people who find themselves alone and lonely in their consumerist lifestyle, but God is not selling a franchised Christianity that comforts us with a set of ethics that our culture predisposes us to accept. The gospel is not an asset we might consider adding to our portfolio of policies and investments. It does not fit nicely into the commercial cult whose own precepts seem written on tablets of stone. Christ proclaims that to live is to serve and he turns the tables on the cult and on the status quo of my life. Discipleship of Christ turns out to be more like battling through 50-foot waves in a leaky boat with a bunch of misfits than a round of golf with some agreeable companions. A handful of misfits may bring in the kingdom, but no matter how large its membership a golf club never will.

There is no issue in society, including the question of what it means to follow Christ day after day and decision after decision, that is not a choice between having and serving, between cult and the counter-cultural commonwealth. The kind of decisions that matter to our planet are those we make in the communities where we live and move and have our being. Charity (an old word for love) begins at home – in our place of belonging, just as it did for the Trinity. I wonder if we have really come to terms with this. It is easy to be so conformed to a world where islands of wealth are surrounded by seas of poverty that we profess faith *in* Jesus without ever applying the faith *of* Jesus to the issues large and small that a powerful minority wish we would leave to them.

## References

Elliott, Larry, *Radical Readings Diary 2003*. London, SCM Press.

Fromm, Erich, *Fear of Freedom*. London, Routledge, 1942.

Hauerwas, Stanley, *The Peaceable Kingdom*. Indiana, University of Notre Dame Press, 1983.

Myers, Ched, *Say To This Mountain*. New York, Orbis Books, 1996.

Neale, Greg, *The Green Travel Guide*. London, Earthscan Publications, 1998.

Williams, Rowan, *Lost Icons*. London, Continuum, 2003.

# 7

# *People Power*

———◦◦◦◦———

*In terms of human relations there will be either one world or
no world.*

(Heschel, 1951)

Recently a woman successfully sued a restaurant in Philadelphia
when she slipped on a soft-drink can and damaged her back. Thirty
seconds before she slipped on the can she had thrown it at her
boyfriend in the heat of an argument. If we find ourselves thinking
'only in America . . .', we should note that during school term-time
Accident and Emergency departments in hospitals in the United
Kingdom are being overrun with children brought in after minor
playground accidents by excessively cautious school staff afraid of
being sued by parents keen to find someone to blame.

We live in a blame culture, though none of us consciously
chose this. It is a by-product of the consumerist society we have
chosen by tick-tack-toe. Consumerism is itself a way of fleeing
from the freedom to which God draws us. Our hearts are restless,
but we try to answer our longings by exercising what passes as
our personal choice. We act as though fulfilment is a product we
can purchase, but lack the personal discernment necessary to
know what really gives us peace. This leads us to make some very
poor decisions, and the wealthier we become the more foolish are
the decisions we can afford. What is to become of a society where
over-eating is a killer disease and liposuction a growing remedy
for those who can pay to have the fat they have consumed sucked
out of their stomachs and thighs?

Fear not only lies behind our poor choices but it also prevents us from admitting our mistakes even when, like Pinocchio's lies, they become as plain as the nose on our face. Accepting the truth is the first step towards forgiveness, but it is one we find hard to take. I think this is the reason for so much of the stress and depression we experience and see in our friends and colleagues. Forgiveness means letting myself off the hook. I prefer to stay on this hook like a fish squirming uncomfortably than admit, like King David, my responsibility for my life and actions. So I look around for someone to blame for my discomfort or I try to justify my decision by extenuating circumstances, claiming in fact that I was powerless to do the good in this situation. In a blame culture we experience ourselves not as people loved and forgiven by God, but as victims.

The extremity of a blame culture is not just a plethora of very wealthy lawyers making money out of a nation of unhappy people. When a group of us blame some other group and refuse to forgive the wrong they have done (or we think they have done) to us over many years or in the distant past, the result is often genocide.

## PAUSE AND REFLECT

Recall a situation in which you found yourself blamed unjustly. How did you feel? What did you do? How important was it to you that the truth be told? What resolved the situation? Now recall a time (perhaps the same situation) when you held someone else to blame for your unhappiness. How did you feel and how strongly did you express your feelings? Note: Genocide is a murderous rage, but Jesus warned against the deadly power of our thoughts. How justified were yours by the facts? The louder we protest our own innocence, the more likely it is in some circumstances that we are hiding some (perhaps minor) share of responsibility that we do not care to admit.

Community is the solution to the blame culture. It is the choice to include, to share power and responsibility, to forgive, and it goes on all the time between husband and wife, parents and children, brothers and sisters, relatives, neighbours, colleagues and friends. In his letter to the Church at Corinth, Paul is inspired in his eloquent and moving description of the love we can have for one another:

> Love is patient and kind; love is not jealous or boastful; it is not arrogant or rude. Love does not insist on its own way; it is not irritable or resentful; it does not rejoice at wrong, but rejoices in the right. Love bears all things, believes all things, hopes all things, endures all things. Love never ends; as for prophecies, they will pass away; as for tongues, they will cease; as for knowledge, it will pass away. For our knowledge is imperfect and our prophecy is imperfect; but when the perfect comes, the imperfect will pass away. When I was a child, I spoke like a child, I thought like a child, I reasoned like a child; when I became a man, I gave up childish ways. For now we see in a mirror dimly, but then face to face. Now I know in part; then I shall understand fully, even as I have been fully understood. So faith, hope, love abide, these three; but the greatest of these is love. (1 Corinthians 13.4–13)

Love like this is what makes the world one. Choosing it returns us to the place where we started (didn't I tell you that God is paradox?), but this time without the need to herd together out of ignorance or instinct or fear. The community that is the source and destination of our journey is a gathering of free individuals in communion with one another and with God.

This is the one world that Heschel recommends – a world where the 'I' of personal choice becomes the 'we' of discernment. Take, for example, our parental right to choose the best education for our children. This is a relatively new but fiercely defended choice in spite of the fact that it can never be a universal right, even in a country like Britain. Some will be able to choose the 'best' school because this establishment, driven to enter the contest for position in performance tables, will select those children most likely to help it maintain that position. The school cannot afford to choose a child who fails the entry criteria, and he or she then has no choice but to attend a less successful school. The absolute right of some to choose, when exercised, actually robs others of even the little choice they have. A group of individual parents might exercise this right, but a discerning community of parents could not possibly do so because community means moving over to make room for other people's children.

God makes room for all your hopes and dreams, your loving decisions and your fearful ones. And wants you to move over too. In Isaiah we read this good advice: 'Widen the space of your tent, stretch out your hangings freely, lengthen your ropes, make your pegs firm; for you will burst out to right and left' (Isaiah 54.2, Jerusalem Bible). It was a promise of compassionate forgiveness for the people of Israel, a future so fertile it would wipe out the shame and misery of their long exile. To us it promises that forgiveness and community will redeem us from our fears, connect us to others, and liberate within us that one world we are made to enjoy.

Widening the space of one's tent is a lovely metaphor for the grace of forgiveness, and living in community is impossible without it. To forgive myself I have to make room for the truth that it was I who made the wrong choice in a situation and/or for the wrong reasons. Truth and reconciliation take me to the threshold of liberation, but the blame culture may make one last attempt to keep me captive by suggesting that since I am to blame, I deserve to suffer the consequences of my action for ever. God, however, is already forgetting what my sin was. Jesus on the cross puts my mistakes in their proper perspective, setting me free when he prays: 'Father, forgive them; for they know not what they do' (Luke 23.34).

Making room for the truth that we are drawn by love and driven by fear can help us to reconcile ourselves to the many mistakes we make. Most of them happen because we really don't know what we are doing. Once we establish our own sinfulness in these terms, we find it less of a shock when other people do or say things that cause us pain. They don't know what they are doing either.

## PAUSE AND REFLECT

If there is someone you cannot forgive it may be useful to use the prayer of Jesus on the cross, 'Father, forgive them; for they know not what they do' (Luke 23.34), as you recall the hurtful scenes of this relationship one by one. Ask Jesus to show you what it was that this person did not know. What did they not know about you and about the situation? What did they not know about themselves and their own fears? A person can know exactly what to say to cause us the greatest pain, but he or she rarely realizes that they are actually attacking in us something that they are afraid of in themselves. And few people attack us out of malice. They may have had every intention to hurt us, but we need to make room for the fact that this is usually an aggressive reaction to their own unrecognized terrors.

Widening the circle of compassion means making room for the many mistakes we and others make. It is the establishing of a community of forgiveness that brings the truth to light, not to apportion blame but to reconcile ourselves to it. We cannot change what is in the past, but through prayer God can gradually change the way we think about it in the present. If we are willing to give up the satisfaction that resentment gives us (and our blame culture tells us is our right), God will give us in its place the grace to pray for those who have hurt us just as Jesus prayed for us on the cross.

As we decide to forgive rather than blame, to make room rather than defend our corner, we become more than isolated individuals participating in various interest groups within the blame culture. We become members together of God's community of peace.

The Church is called to be a model of that community; a tent with pegs firmly imbedded in compassion, and ropes and hangings stretched freely. If she has been, like the women Isaiah addresses, a long time barren, perhaps it is because she is faithful to a patriarchal God interested less in love and more in questions of morality and the preservation of the status quo. This has exiled her from the creative hub of life to a battened-down existence on the parochial sidelines where her humiliation is complete. Few even bother to listen when the Church speaks against war and want, because her behaviour on issues closer to home and hearth are so inhospitable and often downright inhumane.

Recently the Church of Scotland decided to form a national committee to look at the way forward. The committee was called 'A Taskforce for Change'. The Church then decided on 36 men for this task and one woman. While you catch your breath, let me also tell you that the group consisted almost entirely of ordained ministers. I guess the Church of Scotland would recognize its call to be a community, but here we see it operating more like a group. A group brings together a representative number of individuals to collaborate on an issue. A community knows that presence rather than representation is the prerequisite for discernment. Even as a group, the Taskforce for Change is a poor show. Though the ratio of women to men sitting in the pews is 2:1, and though women elders and ministers have served the Church for nearly 40 years, the group is male in gender and masculine in its strategy. No change there then. A community could never have allowed this absence not only of women, but of lay men and lay women, without asking, 'Where are our sisters? Where are our lay people? How can we hope to discern a way forward for the whole community unless we gather the whole community together for this important discernment? How can we show love that "does not insist on its own way" while being so "arrogant or rude" to think that our male voices are the only ones that need to be heard?'

As those attending courses in Christianity make clear, people long to be called from their isolation as numbers in a blame culture to take up their unique place in a community of the forgiven.

The problem is that being part of a group, even a group of religious people, is a lot easier than becoming members together of a community. This is true whether that group is an assortment of people working on a project or a number of people related by blood or marriage and living under one roof. As an individual in a group, I can be selective about my involvement. I bring to the group my preconceptions and prejudices and I can toss these into any discussion on how we move forward or tackle a problem with little regard for how my position impacts on others. Not for the first time I am reminded of a postcard with the quip: 'Quick, ask a teenager while he still knows everything.' I am sure mine is not the only household where adults and teenagers seem to be living on two different planets, never mind communities. In a group it is the more voluble participants, or the ones with more energy for an argument or a more assertive personality, who tend to win the day.

For the Christian community the challenge is to glimpse (however dimly) God's ongoing creation of a commonwealth, inaugurated through the life, death and resurrection of Jesus; a present reality and a future hope. We co-operate with God's work by living as a community just as the earliest believers did. In Acts we read:

Now the company of those who believed were of one heart and soul, and no one said that any of the things which he possessed was his own, but they had everything in common. And with great power the apostles gave their testimony to the resurrection of the Lord Jesus, and great grace was upon them all. There was not a needy person among them, for as many as were possessors of lands or houses sold them, and brought the proceeds of what was sold and laid it at the apostles' feet; and distribution was made to each as any had need. (Acts 4.32–5)

To become a community takes a lot of hard work. As members of a community we deliberately choose not to fight our own corner. Just as the early disciples held their possessions in common, so we try to hold everyone's opinions on an issue in common. While in a group your view is only of value if it agrees with mine, in a community your view *is* mine and mine is yours, no matter how different they are. This grace calls for some restraint because we all are inclined to defend our own views either overtly with aggressive (or passive-aggressive) gestures, language, arguments or, more subtly, by spinning the truth or making jokes. It takes the hard work of honest and persistent prayer to discover and acknowledge to ourselves the baggage we bring and the hidden agendas that are stuffed into that baggage. As I become aware of my own 'stuff', I need God's help to put some or all of it aside for the benefit of the common good. As a result of this effort, listening to others becomes more important than hearing myself talk.

A Christian community wishing to make a discerned decision must be a community of people for whom individual discernment is a way of life. This is stating the obvious, but it is also the most difficult prerequisite to satisfy. We talk a good talk, but few communities are made up of people who pray as though life depended on it.

Assuming that our community is indeed full of discerning people, then it will be helpful to identify what it is that unites us as individuals and makes us a community. What common vocation has the Holy Spirit charged us with?

When the Nazis invaded Denmark the clergy gathered, panic-stricken, in the home of Bishop Hendrik Kraemar, saying 'What should we do?' He told them, 'The first thing to do is ask ourselves who are we? When we know who we are, then we will know what to do.' Following this example, the Church of Scotland might discover that in common with all other Christians its vocation is to be what Elisabeth Schüssler Fiorenza calls in her book *In Memory of Her* 'a discipleship of equals' (Schüssler Fiorenza, 1996); of men and women, boys and girls, who respond to the invitation of Jesus 'follow me' (Mark 2.14).

One of the first things for the community to discern is a way of expressing this vocation verbally that has the agreement of everyone. For example, the Church of Scotland could agree to be this 'discipleship of equals' serving Christ in local parishes throughout Scotland, but a congregation or community might have its own verbal expression of how best to situate the charism in their particular locality. My local congregation is a gathering of people from several rural communities scattered over 100 square miles. For over ten years the congregation has travelled round the villages to worship. We are called to be the people 'walking in pilgrimage, united in faith'. Agreement is necessary because the verbal expression is not just a set of words without power or consequence. It becomes the tool we will use to discern what we will do as a community.

## PAUSE AND REFLECT

Identify some of the groups you participate in and what communities you belong to at this time. Do any of the communities act like groups? How does your community express its shared vocation in concrete terms? Has it thought about this, prayed about it, and come to a consensus? There is no need for anything discerned to be written in stone of course. A tentative decision about who you are as a community will confirm itself or require further consideration as you live together with your task and gain some experience of how it works out in the here and now of action.

Knowing who we are together helps us discern what we should be doing. Then, just as for individual discernment, we need to have among us a shared commitment to put into action the decisions reached through communal discernment. It is a common thing for us to say to God 'show me your will', but then decide ourselves whether or not to accept it. A bit like looking at one's horoscope and, finding it unsatisfactory, turning to another newspaper or magazine in the hope of finding there a more attractive option for the day. In a group, even a Cabinet in government, it is not unusual for one or two people to walk away when the decision reached does not accord with their wishes. This opt-out clause is not available in a discerning community. It won't be needed either. When a community discerns, the prayer continues until the community is at peace with the decision. I can be at peace even when my reservations have not all been allayed because the peace of Christ comes from God and not from my fevered brain. Perhaps an example of a less than perfect discernment process might help.

Nine years ago when our present congregation invited my husband Jack to be their minister we had to decide whether or not to move ourselves and our three young children from the central belt of Scotland to rural Aberdeenshire. The initial response of Jack and the three children was 'Let's go for it!' I was equally unequivocal – 'Not on your life.'

There followed a time of very necessary information gathering. We had to investigate schools, the viability of the small congregation, the condition of the accommodation, the prospect of work in the area for me, public transport, recreational amenities, and various other practicalities. Next we did the 'column exercise' together (mentioned in Chapter 4). In this case, since the decision was between 'accept' or 'don't accept', we had four columns headed 'Accept – reasons for', 'Accept – reasons against', 'Reject – reasons for', 'Reject – reasons against'. It took some time to tease out all the issues. We quickly listed the obvious reasons for accepting and those for rejecting, but we had to dig a little deeper into ourselves to notice and allow to come to light our reasons against accepting and our reasons against rejecting. Once the columns seemed to reflect all the hopes and fears of the family we tried to give each entry a weight in the light of our shared insights into the faith of Christ and the call of his gospel to our family. This led us to make a tentative decision and we then took this individually to prayer, sharing our insights between times of prayer until a growing sense of settled peace surrounded the choice. We shared our tentative decision with a few close friends and family and this deepened our peace. The outcome of the discernment was a decision to move to Aberdeenshire.

No surprise there, then, you might be thinking – the husband wanted the position and the wife was brought round. But I assure you that my 'Not on your life' was in many ways the one more likely to carry the day. It was the status quo and this gave it a weight. God does not go in for change for change's sake and in fact we need to guard against the temptation to escape from the ordinary into something more glamorous or novel. My viewpoint was expressed out of concern for our children and I tend to be the partner who represents our children's welfare in decisions like this. Then, too, the nature of our marital relationship means that I tend to get my own way (not always for the best) – partly because when it comes to debating an issue, I am a little more driven than my husband is to win any argument. Also, Jack's 'Let's go for it' had its own mixture of motives, romanticism, escapism, inappropriate self-denial, etc. so that though his initial response turned out to be our final choice, it looked a lot different for him by the end of the discernment process. Our 'stuff' – my driven-ness, my fierce mothering, and lots more along with Jack's own concerns – none of it is a problem unless it remains hidden and therefore powerfully able to control our communal discernment.

Think of a decision that your community might usefully discern. In church this could be the advisability of taking out the pews to allow more flexible seating. In the family it could be the decision to take an elderly relative into your home. A friend of mine has always been against putting elderly parents in a resi-dential home. He thinks it's just one more example of a society believing that nothing should be allowed to restrict the freedom of the individual. But recently when faced with his own aged father needing care, my friend found that he had a dilemma. How can I take him to live with me when all the work would fall on my wife's shoulders? Both husband and wife work, but the woman works only part-time.

Who knows what the answer is. Not me. If there was one answer to this question that applied to every concerned family and to every aged relative, either expressing a desire to move in or being unable to let their wishes known, life would be simpler – though less free. The couple need to seek God's grace to be as available as possible to God's preference for them all in this situation. Then they would find it useful to list the reasons for taking father home, and those reasons that make this impossible, the reasons a residential home would be the best decision, and the reasons that make this a bad idea. A careful weighting of each observation they make will assist towards a tentative decision. This decision can then be placed before God in prayer for a period of time suitable to the importance of the matter and the consequences of the decision. They are looking for a sense of peace about the decision and they must both experience this. It would be useful to guard against a euphoric feeling that masquerades as peace, but is unreal.

Peace does not have to be completely tranquil or always certain for it to be authentic. Peace comes from Jesus and it was he who turned the tables upside down in the Temple. Sometimes he does this with other things too. I believe when we decide to include everyone, we discover that this is what God is doing; that this is the gospel. The God who answers prayer with a question, 'What if?', is shockingly fertile. No matter how creative or liberal we think we are, she is more so – and, for the sake of the commonwealth of unity, will continue to move over and make room for the most surprising developments. Perhaps my friends will decide that he can work part-time and look after his father while she works full-time.

## PAUSE AND REFLECT

Whatever decision your community wants to make, try this simple exercise to spot some relational 'stuff' that might obstruct discernment if it goes undetected.

Look at the question and imagine in turn one member of the community after the other posing the question out of his or her own concern that indeed action needs to be taken (e.g. the pews should come out or the relative should move in). Notice your gut response to the question as it comes from this person. Then move on and imagine the same question put by another member, noting your response to the question and the questioner. When you have considered each member of the community, notice in what ways your initial response to the question varied, depending on who said it and which button it pressed in you.

Sometimes we give our gut response to a person or suggestion a weight or significance that it does not merit. If we then start debating from this prejudiced position, we will be doing something other than Christian discernment. We will be saying to God – 'this is my will' rather than 'show me your will'. This unhelpful attitude can be avoided by praying for the grace to be drawn beyond our individual personalities and the chemistry between them. So when a question arises in your community that requires a decision, give everyone a chance to state their initial response quietly and respectfully. Then each person should go away and pray for the grace to be available to God's choice for this community and to want this more than they want to impress anyone or score points off another member.

Once that stuff is cleared away, or at the very least you are aware of it and therefore can work hard to compensate and bring yourself back to a point of equilibrium – 'not what I will, but what thou wilt' (Mark 14.36) – then you can gather together to begin the discernment process, with a deep awareness of the common vocation that is your unity and the agreement to make the concrete verbal expression of this the touchstone for that discernment. You will find what you seek: God who is transforming this world, not through Taskforces for Change, nor through individual agendas, but through the communion of saints, the body of Christ.

It is especially important in a family to involve children as much as possible in decisions that affect their lives either directly or indirectly. They will learn what a community is by living in a community and having their say as one among equals. It is also important to let them choose the level of their involvement. A four-year-old may be happy to state a voluble opinion. A seven-year-old may have lots of questions that need answering. A fourteen-year-old comes charged with hormones that react explosively to any adult foolish enough to be in the same room, never mind the same discussion.

If the Church is the model of God's commonwealth, then these family communities are the building blocks. Widening the space of this particular tent may mean conceiving a new way of being 'family'. Can we make room to include and empower and receive forgiveness from couples of the same gender who want to commit themselves to a loving relationship, take care of one another in sickness as well as in health for as long as they live? I hope so, and I would like to see the Church family lead the way in this step from the blame culture to the commonwealth.

The number of divorces could be reduced by a Church that helps couples discern whether this person is the right partner with whom to create a new community. Already we see marriage preparation classes and these facilitate useful consideration of important issues. The Church could also facilitate the couple's discernment of what unites them as individuals and makes them potentially a community.

## PAUSE AND REFLECT

The wedding business is almost as big as the tourism business and it is easy to forget that living as a married couple is about serving God's world, not making one for ourselves. Those contemplating marriage, and those wishing to reform an established marriage, may find it helpful to reflect together on the uniqueness of the community their marriage will inaugurate. What common vocation is the Holy Spirit charging us with? How might we express this vocation in the marriage vows we take? In what ways can we make room for the concrete expression of this shared vocation in our daily lives together?

Marriage makes a community from two unrelated people and their families. It is not to be undertaken lightly as though community is something we can walk away from. God did not suck it and see when he chose the people of Israel for a special relationship with him. He chose to covenant himself to them and this promise was the foundation of the relationship. Once a couple have discerned the charism of their relationship, the marriage ceremony becomes the place where they covenant themselves to one another and to it. By God's grace they will discover that love and fidelity, not only to a person but to the relationship and to its purpose as a building block of the commonwealth, is the key to a good marriage.

Imagine a whole community turning out to offer support to a couple when resolving to be the kind of family community that serves the common weal through inclusive love. Wouldn't it be great to see bigger celebrations of births, deaths and marriages with more friends and neighbours attending, and less lavish catering arrangements? The more we get together to laugh, to cry, to welcome a new life or give thanks for a life passed, the more opportunity we have to practise being that one world that

Heschel recommends. The more frequently we rub up against the relative or neighbour who irks us, the more likely we will learn to rub along well together. Only when we make room for all kinds of folk can we learn how to be a community of forgiven people.

## References

Heschel, Abraham Joshua, *Man Is Not Alone: A Philosophy of Religion*. New York, Noonday Press, Farrar, Straus and Giroux, 1951.

Schüssler Fiorenza, Elisabeth, *In Memory of Her*. London, SCM Press, 1996.

# 8

# *To Be or Not to Be*

*When we know who we are it becomes clear that we are called
to lay that person on the line as part of the solution to this
world's problems. God is working on wholeness still, and now
we are in a position to work with God on the wholeness not of
our individual selves, or of a group of individuals like the
church, but on the holiness of creation.*

(Holt, 2002)

Do you remember my friend Alan's difficulty with restaurant
menus? Imagine turning up at your favourite restaurant, asking
for the menu, and being directed to a board in the corner of the
room on which is written: 'Soup of the Day'. You might be
surprised, wonder what has gone wrong in the kitchen, feel
aghast at the idea of paying an extravagant price for a bowl of
soup. Curiosity may prompt you to enquire what particular
soup was being offered that day. Whether it turned out to be a
firm favourite or something entirely new to your palate, feeling
cheated of a choice, you are unlikely to order it. When we are
accustomed to à la carte, Soup of the Day can look like nothing.

Not far from where I live there is a restaurant like this. It
accommodates only a small number of patrons in one evening and
there is no menu at all. Instead, the chef arrives at the table to tell
the guests what he is making for them. His choice, made earlier in
the day, depends on what fresh meat, fish, vegetables and fruit he
takes delivery of from the surrounding farms and markets.

Quality, not choice, is the experience on offer. Of course, the chef could prepare lots of excellent meals, but he prefers to produce one to perfection, using only the best ingredients and giving it his full attention. Sounds good, doesn't it? The ideal restaurant for Alan and me to choose when we want to enjoy each other's company.

Freedom can seem like a vast à la carte menu of options for our life. The good news of Christ's gospel is that real freedom is not so much about breadth of choice as about the courage to be chosen. At least, that's what Jesus found. He was God's chosen one; being the Christ was the one vocation that made complete sense of his life. And being our true selves turns out to be the one choice that will make sense of our lives too. In the same way that Alan cannot enjoy his meal until he chooses what to eat, and cannot choose one thing without forgoing the alternatives, Christ's gospel invites us to make the choice of one from many. If God is moving over to make room for a commonwealth of free and responsible beings, then the decisions that matter are the ones I make to become my real, unique and irreplaceable self in that peaceful community.

Jesus was the most real person who ever lived. Through the choices he made, Jesus discovered his identity as the Christ and he lived this with single-minded devotion. This meant denying himself the many options for the one that was real and really mattered. So it is with some feeling that he tells his disciples: 'If any man would come after me, let him deny himself and take up his cross and follow me' (Mark 8.34).

## PAUSE AND REFLECT

If I were a Life Coach, I might ask you what you have done in the last ten years, in pursuit of whatever goal in life you have made your own. Christ asks what choices you have denied yourself in order to follow him. There is a great deal of inappropriate denial that goes on among Christians – try to identify this by asking his question in this form: 'What choices have you denied yourself in order to follow me in my pursuit of the real you?'

The idea that we should consider denying ourselves anything is counter-cultural. To be is to shop; to be alive is to have, and we are constantly told that we can have whatever we want, whenever we want it. Even eternal youth is within our grasp at a price if we are prepared to undergo the surgery necessary to lift and tuck the years away. What nonsense this all becomes when we understand that to be fully alive is to be my true self serving others.

Then I can forgo the alternatives, however attractive these seem. And these can seem very attractive. Not declaring who we really are has its advantages. We can be whoever others want us to be or imagine us to be. This will not give us peace, but peace-and-quiet can seem a reasonable substitute.

## PAUSE AND REFLECT

'Who do you say that I am?' (Luke 9.20) Jesus asked his companions. Imagine how Jesus felt about the responses he received. Imagine yourself asking this question of the people around you. What answers do you think they would give and how does each different image of you make you feel? Take the exercise further, if you dare, by actually asking friends, family and colleagues for a one-word description of you. Be prepared for some surprises (especially from the very young and the very wise) and notice how you feel about these and also about the more expected responses. Come back to prayer and address the question to Jesus. Who does he say you are?

Jesus knew who he was, and being true to this meant denying himself the option of being all things to all men. Some wanted him to be their healer, and though he healed this was not his calling. Some wanted him to be their teacher, and though he taught them this was not his vocation. Some wanted him for their

Messiah, but the Christ he discovered within was very different from the Messiah they wanted him to be: someone to deliver Israel from the might of Rome. The Christ that was real for Jesus was the Human One who serves a commonwealth of peace and blazes a trail that will lead us through our trials to the goal of our quest; the truth of our identity lived in unity with God for ever.

Imagine two lovers sitting together on a seat. In fact, there are actually six 'characters' present. There is the man as he actually is and the woman as she actually is. Then there is the man's idea of the woman and the woman's idea of the man, along with his idea of himself and her idea of herself. No wonder relationships are complex! This confusion of personas in a relationship has one thing going for it. The man can be himself, can be the person she wants him to be, can be the person he fondly imagines himself to be. This multiple choice relieves him of the responsibility of being single-minded. It also removes the limitations that single-mindedness or integrity places on his freedom. The same applies to the woman.

In prayer we often petition for 'the grace of our Lord Jesus Christ'. The grace Jesus had, and we are seeking, was nothing more or less than the courage to limit his life to those actions that were authored by his real identity. Jesus never went anywhere. Unlike Paul, who made great journeys, Jesus limited his audience to those within 60 miles of Nazareth. He never wrote anything, limiting the impact of his message to those of a particular time as well as place. He could have been a missionary. He could have been a writer. Instead, for little more than three years, he was the Christ.

Telling a story by a lake to a crowd hungry for direction; Jesus is the Christ. Transforming water into wine at a family wedding; Jesus is the Christ. Sweating blood in the Garden of Gethsemane at the prospect of a violent and humiliating death; Jesus is the Christ. Forgiving you and me for all the violence and lies we choose and then deny responsibility for; Jesus is the Christ. Dying for his faith in God's quest and ours; Jesus is the Christ. Appearing to his disciples when they thought death had robbed them of the choice to follow him; Jesus is the Christ: the Human One.

Being really human has its risks. No matter how ordinary your looks and stature, if you are real you will stand out in a crowd. There is, and always will be, only one of you. So you are bound to be noticed. Real people attract attention and, though this may begin pleasantly enough, Christ's passion reminds us that the crowd can turn hostile as soon as your integrity makes them uncomfortably aware of how phony they are being. They don't know what they are doing, of course, but though this fact may help us to forgive, it does not remove the pain we will suffer at their hands. In the most difficult circumstances when we doubt God's love and very existence and cry out in despair, 'Where is God in all of this mess?' or 'Why hast thou forsaken me?' (Mark 15.34), the answer remains constant. God is present at the very centre of this world's chaos and our own personal chaos; not orchestrating, but accompanying us through the darkest of places. He/she labours continuously with everything that life is and does to us, helping us discover in it all the very essence of our own souls' being and of Being.

Not many of us will lose our lives for the sake of this endeavour, though in every generation some do. Gandhi, Martin Luther King and the Salvadoran Archbishop Oscar Romero come to mind as well as Jesus himself. We may, however, find ourselves laying down what we think our life is as we follow Jesus to a Jerusalem that is our trial as much as his. There we soon discover that God so loves the story of the Christ choosing to die rather than betray his identity, and the love from which this sprang, that God repeats it in anyone willing to follow Christ's example of faith.

At the very least this means denying ourselves those other dishes. Sanctity or wholeness consists in being yourself. This may mean standing out when we are more accustomed to melting into the background. For many it means dying to some fantasy about life. These vary from person to person, but are all variations on a theme: I am really a prince/princess stolen at birth and now waiting to be rescued and established in the lifestyle that is my due. We flirt with fantasy and do not notice that it prevents us from experiencing and enjoying what is real and present to us.

The more we fantasize, the less substantial we become. We make decisions that are immaterial to God's decision to create, and with smoke and mirrors make these seem clever or expedient. Remember Tolkien's Frodo and the powerful ring? Whenever he slipped the ring on his finger he became invisible. This felt good. It gave him an advantage over others and could get him out of trouble. However, the more he wore the ring the less well he felt. Over time, he began to feel stretched and thin and strangely unconnected to the real world. The power of the ring began to cast a shadow over him even when he wasn't wearing it, pulling him inexorably into the darkness. It became increasingly difficult to think of giving the ring away. The fantasy we are in thrall to is powerful, like that ring. Giving it up can feel like death.

We may think this is a poor show. We are so used to pretending to be who we are not, slipping from one role to another in the variety of circumstances we encounter each day, that we cannot imagine living differently. We have so little idea of the depth of reality to be discovered in our true selves that we cannot imagine it satisfying ourselves or those around us for very long.

On the contrary, being real turns out to be the one choice that will make sense of our lives. It is resurrection, life out of death, and it is eternal. We will never tire of being real because our personal identity will always surprise us, always satisfy, always have meaning, and always draw us to further depths of meaning as God's quest for unity with us continues. Our personal identity turns out to be the Soup of the Day. To choose it is to begin to delve into the mystery and meaning of our wonderful selves; the being that Being lets-be.

I hope this prospect inspires you. I hope you are excited at the idea of becoming a discerning member of a marriage, a family, a community, by first discerning and beginning to savour your own 'veriness' (Heschel, 1951). If so, you will find my earlier book, *Listening to the Soul*, a useful companion as you seek to confirm or discover who you really are in much the same way that Jesus discovered this for himself. It will liberate you to love the Lord your God with all your heart, soul and mind, and your neighbour as yourself. This quest for the unique essence of our being is the only authentic task in life.

Soon after writing that book, I packed away my word processor, told myself that giving spiritual direction and writing books about it could not possibly be anything more than a pastime, and became the administrator of a charitable trust. The work was interesting and worthwhile, using some of the skills I had developed in earlier employment. Though I was neither inspired by the charity nor the tasks of an administrator, the salary was useful at a time when my eldest son was applying for university courses to pursue his vocation. I did the job efficiently and gratefully – honourably, I hope – but without passion. It was not life-giving to me but it was expedient. However, I discovered that, willing as I was to give up my own decision to become fully human in order to facilitate my children's becoming, this would not do.

One day a man came into the office to discuss some business of the trust. He had read my first book and enquired after the second. I told him the subject matter and he began to describe his own struggle to choose between what was life-giving for him and what was the expected thing. I gave him a few rules of thumb for discernment and he was grateful. I, however, was agitated for the rest of the day. For a few minutes while I encouraged this man to be true to himself, I was living. As he left and I turned my attention to columns of figures, I knew I was only 'surviving' in my current job. Arriving home at the end of the day I burst into my husband's study and exclaimed irritably, 'Why is God tormenting me?' I meant, 'Why does God not leave me alone to do what I have to do? Why does he/she persist in leaping like a baby in the womb at every opportunity?' In the space of a heartbeat my husband replied: 'Because he loves you very much.' The child leapt again. Bother. You see, I am not an administrator. I was not born to administer the kingdom or follow the path of expediency.

Sometimes we lose our way. Sometimes we find ourselves at a

loss to understand what it means for us to be real. When the toy Rabbit, in Margery Williams's moving story *The Velveteen Rabbit* asks the old Skin Horse what 'Real' is he wonders if it means having bells and whistles like some of the newer toys in the nursery. The Skin Horse tells him that Real is nothing to do with how you are made. It is a thing that happens to a toy when a child loves it very much for a long, long time. Real is something you become.

The Rabbit asks if the process is painful and if it happens all at once, like the wind-up toys he sees springing into action, or gradually over time. The Skin Horse admits that it can be a long and painful process, remembering that by the time the Boy's Uncle made him Real, all his fine horse-hair had been loved off and his joints loosened. He observes that becoming Real rarely happens to toys that break easily or need to be carefully kept and only looked at in their display cabinet. Toys that cannot be played with too enthusiastically remain only toys.

God is making us real through a love both personal and enthusiastic. By interacting with us and with every decision we make, God hopes to help us become truly human and freely part of God. For what matters to God is that, like Christ, we are free to make creative decisions that affirm others and unite us to them without any loss of individuality. God knows that freedom like this overcomes our separateness and all our fears. It is the kingdom come.

## References

Heschel, Abraham Joshua, *Man Is Not Alone: A Philosophy of Religion*. New York, Noonday Press, Farrar, Straus and Giroux, 1951.

Holt, Sandra, *Listening to the Soul*. London, SPCK, 2002.

# Acknowledgements

Extracts from the following are reproduced by permission.

David L. Fleming, SJ, *The Spiritual Exercises of Saint Ignatius: A Literal Translation and A Contemporary Reading.* Used with permission: © The Institute of Jesuit Sources, St Louis, MO. All rights reserved.

Erich Fromm, *The Fear of Freedom,* Routledge, 1942. Used with permission.

Stanley Hauerwas, *The Peaceable Kingdom,* University of Notre Dame Press, 1983. Used with permission.

Abraham Joshua Heschel, 'One God' and 'The Essence of Man' from *Man is Not Alone: A Philosophy of Religion.* Copyright © 1951 by Abraham J. Heschel. Copyright renewed 1979 by Sylvia Heschel. Reprinted by permission of Farrar, Straus and Giroux, LLC.

Mother Julian of Norwich, *Revelations of Divine Love.* Reproduced by permission of Hodder and Stoughton Limited.

Søren Kierkegaard, *Sickness unto Death,* Princeton University Press, 1954. Used with permission.

Anthony de Mello, SJ, *Contact with God,* Gujarat Sahitya Prakash, 1990. Used with permission.

Rowan Williams, *Lost Icons,* Continuum, 2003. Used with permission.